THEN & NOW

HARPERS FERRY

OPPOSITE: When people think of Harper's Ferry, they automatically think of John Brown and his ill-fated raid of 1859, and rightly so. Prior to that raid, the town was barely on the map. However, because of that raid, the town became a hot seat of American history. The raid became a catalyst for the Civil War, and our country was changed forever, for the better. (Courtesy of Harpers Ferry National Historical Park [HFNHP].)

THEN & NOW

HARPERS FERRY

Dolly Nasby

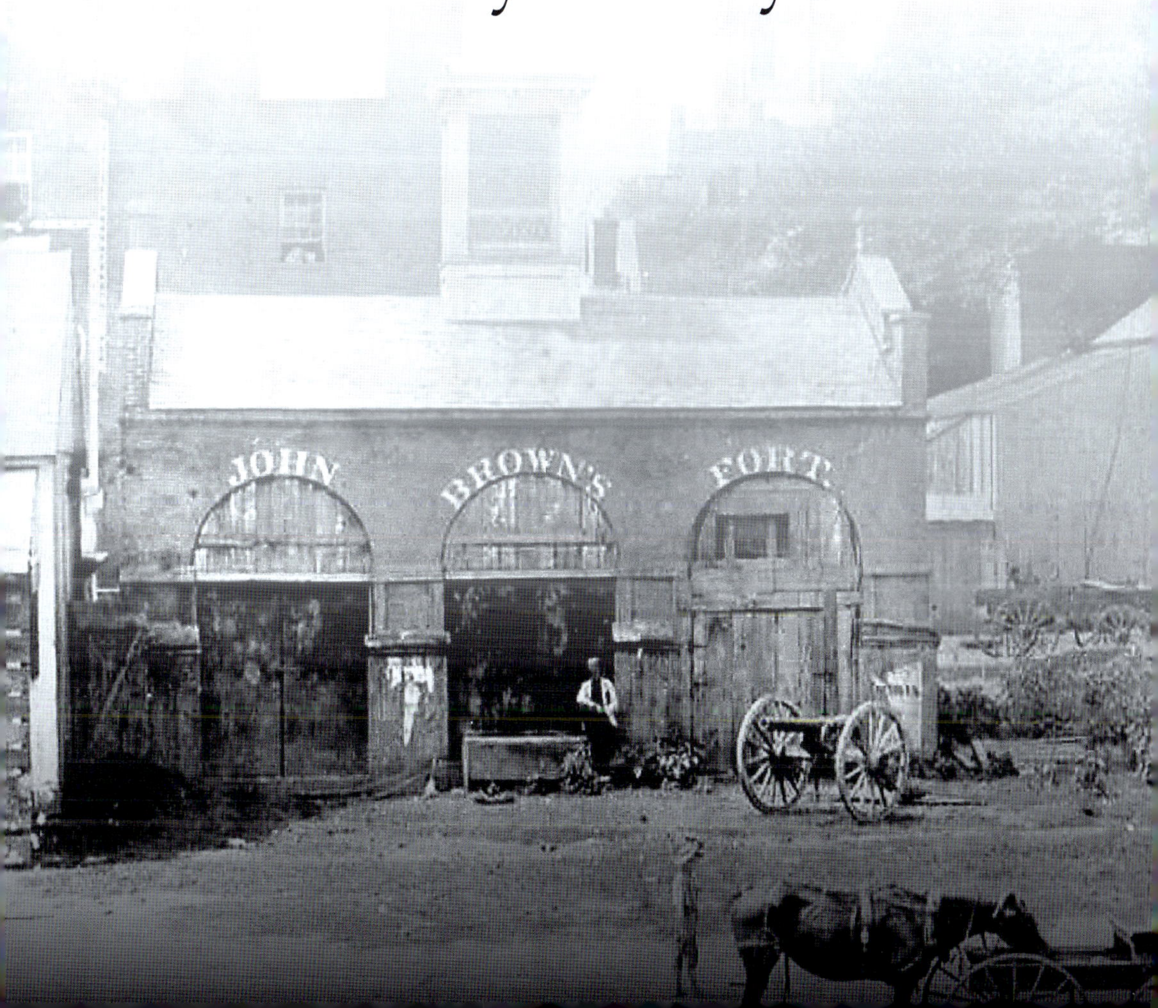

It is with great joy that I dedicate this book to my precious grandchildren, Emily and Stephen. They are the light of my life and my best playmates. I hope they enjoy the book and learn something. I was a teacher before I became an author, so there will be a quiz in three weeks' time. You better start reading and taking notes!

ISBN 978-0-7385-4414-4

Library of Congress Control Number: 2006937912

Published by Arcadia Publishing
Charleston, South Carolina

Printed in the United States of America

Then and Now is a registered trademark and is used under license from Salamander Books Limited

For all general information contact Arcadia Publishing at:
Telephone 843-853-2070
Fax 843-853-0044
E-mail sales@arcadiapublishing.com
For customer service and orders:
Toll-Free 1-888-313-2665

Visit us on the Internet at www.arcadiapublishing.com

On the Front Cover: While the sun sets on the building in the top photograph on the cover, it is not anywhere near setting on the town itself. Harpers Ferry is alive and well, living out her destiny. Begun as a small crossroads at the junction of two often-tumultuous rivers, it has overcome many hardships—John Brown's raid, the Civil War, and floods. Today the town has arisen and shines as a beacon of light for all those seekers of history who want to step back in time and pretend that they are living in another historical era. For those seekers, who prior to their visit here could only imagine what a town in the 1800s would look like, this is their respite. (Courtesy of HFNHP.)

On the Back Cover: Little did the owners of this gas station know how the streets of Harpers Ferry would change. Begun as a crossroads of so many modes of transportation—boats, wagons, horses, and trains—today it serves as a destination. The number of trains that come to town today has decreased from the average of 28 during the town's peak. Tourists today park at Cavalier Heights and catch the shuttle bus into town, where they linger and try to catch a glimpse of life in the 1800s. (Courtesy of HFNHP.)

Contents

Acknowledgments

When a person takes on an endeavor such as this, she really begins by having faith that people will help her along the way, and they usually do. When she begins, she never knows where the road will take her, so she really has to trust others to assist her along the way. She has to follow her nose, which I did.

I have a tremendous sense of gratitude for the help received from Nancy Hatcher and Rich Raymond of the Harpers Ferry National Historical Park. They are experts in their field and tremendously helpful to researchers such as I. Thank you both very much for everything (even the chocolate). All of the vintage photographs in this book were obtained through the Harpers Ferry National Historical Park (HFNHP), and I am very grateful for the use of these images. I also am very grateful that our government sees fit to fund the park service to preserve our valuable history and heritage. All of the modern photographs were taken by me.

Another person who was helpful but did not even know he was helping me was David T. Gilbert. His help was in the form of a book he wrote in 1983 entitled *A Walker's Guide to Harpers Ferry*. It has been printed 13 times and has had 5 editions. It is jam-packed with valuable information and is truly a great resource.

I also would like to thank Arcadia for being such a great publisher. They currently are the leading publisher of local and regional history in the country, and I personally believe that they perform an invaluable service. Major historians, scholars, and authors record our national history; local authors are left to write the local histories, but without a publisher such as Arcadia, we would never have our works published. We are very grateful.

I would also like to thank my parents for instilling in me the love of history, but they have passed away. Hopefully, they knew how grateful I was to have such wonderful parents. And maybe they are looking down and saying, "Awwww, look what Dolly's doing."

And last but never least, I want to thank Walt, my husband of 13 years, my friend, my confidant, who has tolerated many a late dinner and made many trips to the grocery store in my stead when I just did not have the time. And he never grumbled once!

Thank you everyone, very much. Even though my name is on the byline, many people contributed to this project, and I am very thankful.

If you find any errors, please notify me: Dolly Nasby, PO Box 61, Bakerton, WV 25410

INTRODUCTION

When I was a child, I learned to sing "John Brown's body lies a moldin' in the grave." I never really learned the story of John Brown until later in life, and when I did, I was amazed at the courage he and his friends had. To take a stand against slavery at a time when slavery was the status quo was an amazing feat of bravery. Yes, he was eccentric, but without his actions, slavery might have continued for quite a while longer. As it was, it had lasted too long.

Little Harpers Ferry never planned on being in the limelight. When George Stephens founded his ferry here at the Point, he just thought of the town as a jumping-off place for travel farther west. Robert Harper bought "The Hole" from Stephens, and it became known as Harpers Ferry. Both George Washington and Thomas Jefferson visited the little town and loved the countryside.

Pres. George Washington had established the armory and arsenal here, along with another in Springfield, Massachusetts. When he did so, he probably never thought that the little town would become so famous. The residents of Harpers Ferry didn't think so either. It was not a particularly pleasant place to live. It was located right on the edge of two rivers that were very tumultuous at times. The rivers would flood periodically and ruin everything in their paths, leaving behind destruction and disease. But the people of Harpers Ferry were not quitters. They built, rebuilt, and rebuilt again because they would not give up.

They saw the benefit of the waterpower available along the two rivers and established many factories on Virginius Island. Time and time again, the floods would destroy homes and businesses, but the people never gave up. However, after numerous floods and many lost lives, the almost 200 people who either lived on Virginius Island or had factories on the island came to realize that staying was foolish. Eventually, all the factories closed and all residents of the island left, leaving behind only the remnants of their former dwellings and places of business, the foundations of which can be seen today.

The people in the Upper Town fared better because the water of the rivers could not reach them. In the Lower Town, floods caused repeated damage over the years. However, people did not leave; they did not quit but stayed and repaired what was damaged by each flood.

During the Civil War, Harpers Ferry changed hands eight times. Every time the troops left, they took everything of value that they could find with them. The residents eventually left town also. After the war was over and the residents returned, what they found was devastating to them. So many of their buildings and homes had been ransacked or destroyed by squatters. But again, they did not give up; they did not quit but continued to work to repair their little hamlet.

During the 1920s, Harpers Ferry was a thriving little town. It was not big, but within the town, people could find everything they needed to live a normal life—grocery stores, churches, pharmacists, auto mechanics, lawyers, doctors, dentists, and so on. People did not need to leave town.

In 1944, the town was made into a national historical park, and that was the beginning of the reemergence of Harpers Ferry as a prosperous little town. The park began by trying to acquire all the buildings and land that had been part of the town in 1859, the time of John Brown's raid and the event that eventually defined the little town. The goal was to make the Lower Town appear, as closely as possible, as it appeared in 1859. They did it, and they did a good job of it.

Today Harpers Ferry is a place where a visitor can really step back in time and see what it was like in 1859. The buildings appear the same. The sidewalks and roads are uneven, as they would have been then, although they are mostly all paved today. From time to time, period reenactors roam the streets wearing clothing similar to clothing that would have been worn in the 1800s.

In the Upper Town, the Storer College buildings have become park service buildings, where offices and dormitories are now located. Storer College had been established to teach the freedmen (former slaves) after the Civil War. While many people in the town were not in favor of having Storer College within their confines, the school provided a wonderful place for the freed slaves to begin their education in a non-threatening environment. When it was closed in 1955, it was a sad moment. The decision of *Brown v. the Board of Education* unwittingly caused the school to close. After that Supreme Court decision was uttered, the funding Storer College had enjoyed was removed, which meant financially it could not continue. Many Storer graduates still live in Harpers Ferry today.

Today the college buildings are in the Upper Town, and restorations have taken place where needed. Some buildings have been razed, but many important buildings still serve a purpose, some housing the park service offices.

I have divided the book into chapters that deal with central themes. The first chapter, entitled "The Village Down Under: Lower Town," deals with businesses, buildings, and streets in the Lower Town. Chapter two, "Elevated Avenue: High Street," deals with High Street. Many businesses and dwellings were located along this street. "The Maximal Milieu: Upper Town" is chapter three. In chapter four, "Justifiable Pedagogy: Storer College," I included photographs and information about Storer College. Water has played a tremendous role in the life of Harpers Ferry, and that is dealt with in chapter five, entitled "H_2O and Spans: Shenandoah and Potomac Rivers and Bridges." Last but not least, chapter six is called "Elevations in Mary's Land: Maryland Heights" and has pictures of Maryland Heights, the bridges on the Maryland shore, and the Chesapeake and Ohio Canal.

This book is by no way a complete book on Harpers Ferry, neither then nor now. Not all subjects could be covered because photographs were not available on all subjects, and for that I apologize. In addition, I would need much more space than these few pages allow.

CHAPTER 1

The Village Down Under

Lower Town

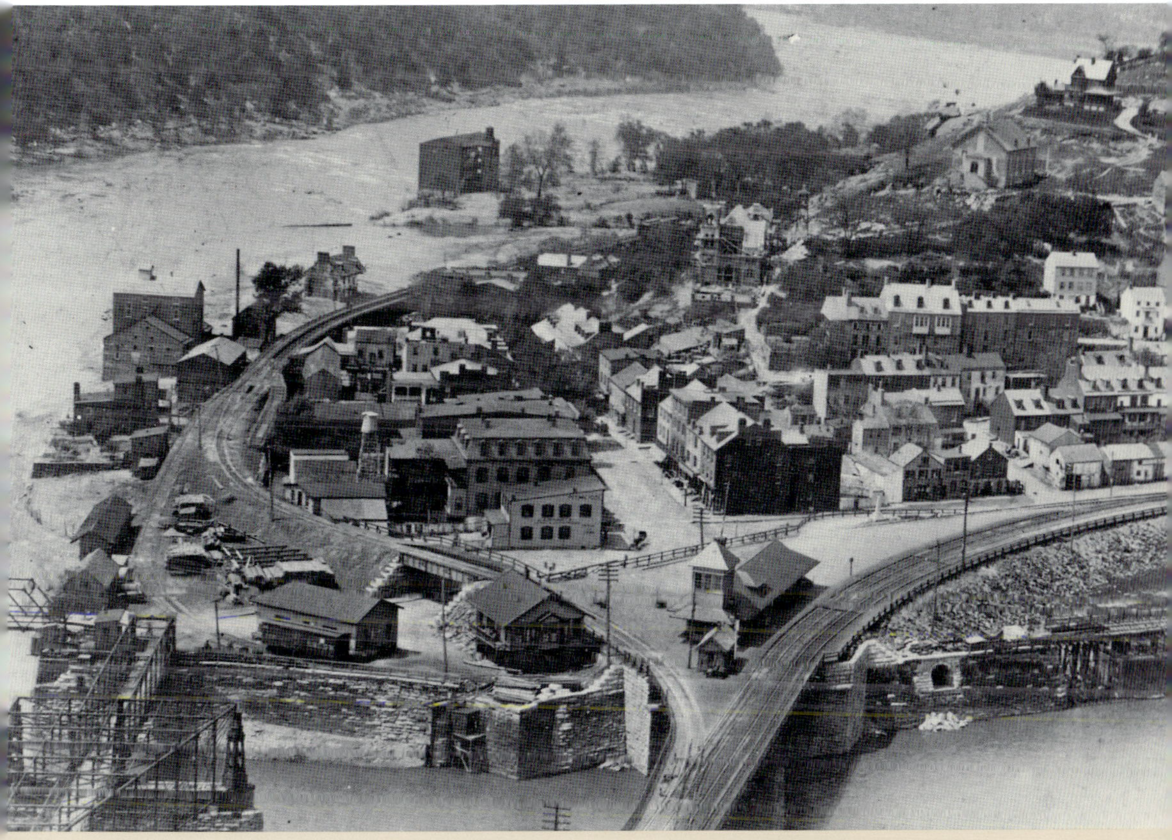

This 1896 photograph clearly shows many buildings in the Lower Town. The Shenandoah River is on the left, and the Potomac River comes in from the right. Every building to the left of the tracks on the Shenandoah side has been removed over time, either by the rivers or by the National Park Service when the town was declared a national historical park, and the NPS has tried to restore it to the year of John Brown's raid. Many visible foundations remain.

Traveling east on Shenandoah Street, to the right rests Virginius Island. It is now devoid of buildings that formerly housed the industrial heart of the town, although the foundations of those buildings are still visible. Straight ahead on the left, an armorer's dwelling is visible. Between 1810 and 1812, seventy-four such dwellings were erected on government property for armorers, at a time when housing was difficult to come by.

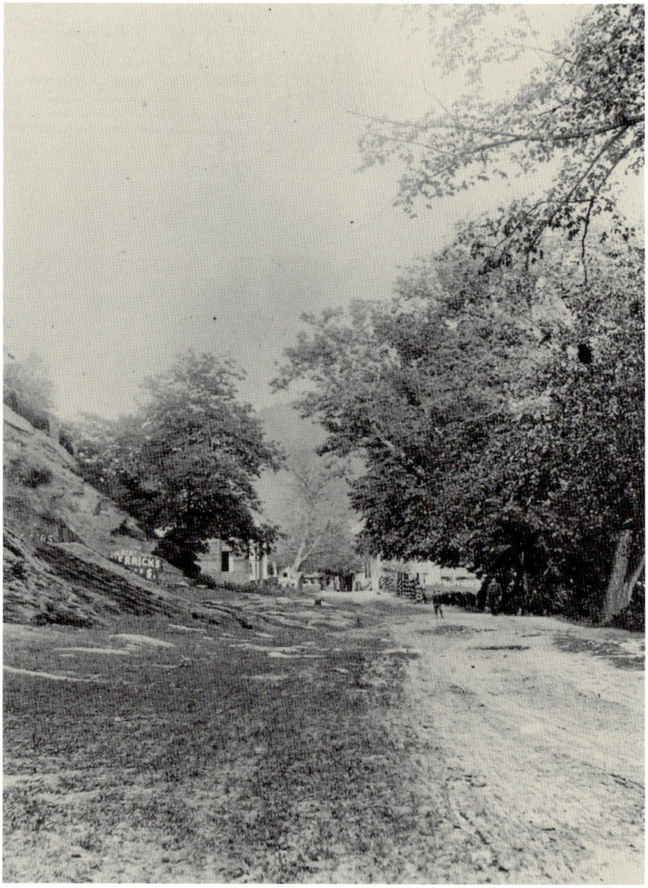

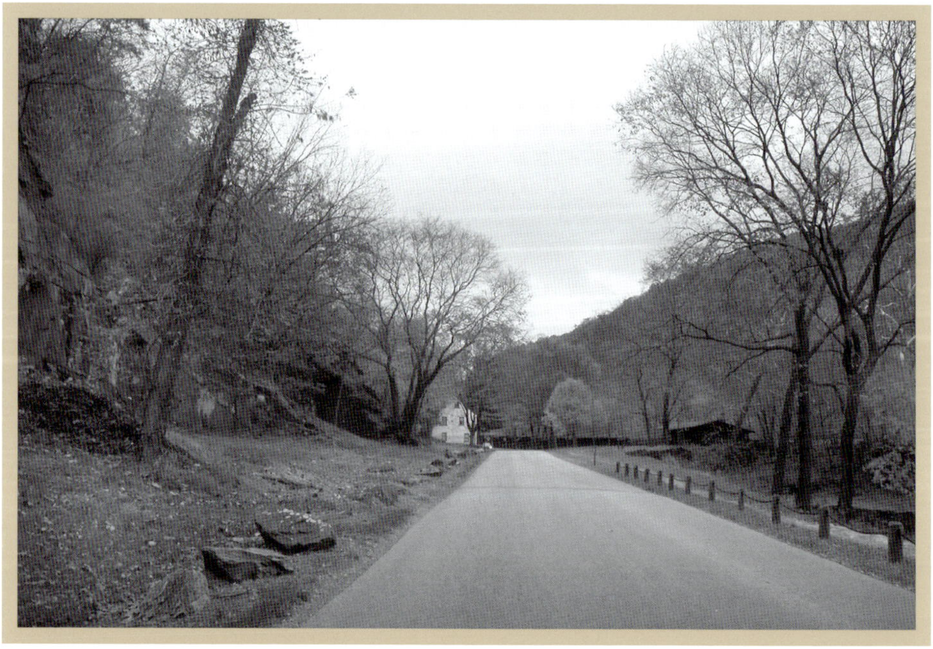

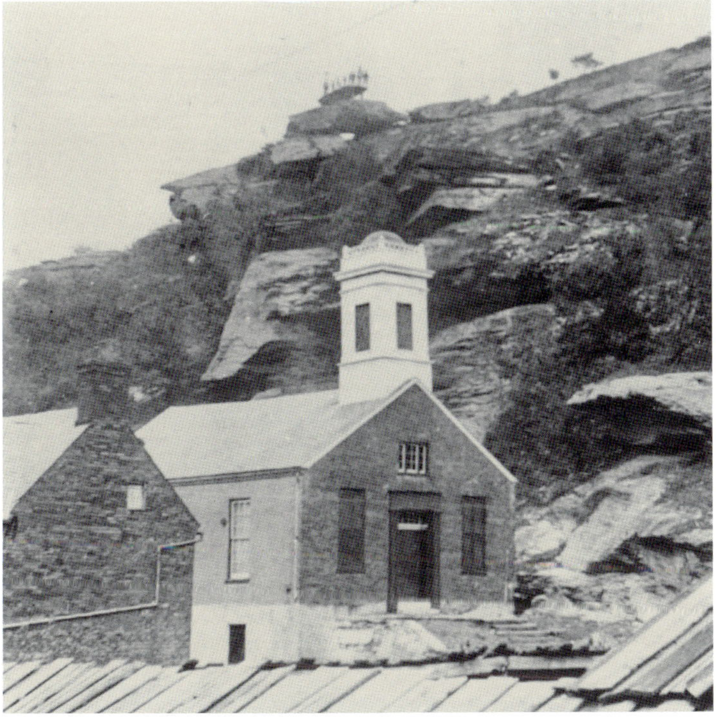

Taken in 1865, the "then" photograph shows both the Presbyterian church and Jefferson Rock high above it. The church was located on Shenandoah Street and faced the Shenandoah River. Today all we see is the foundation. St. Peter's Catholic Church was located directly above it on the hill. The privy of St. Peter's Church caused some health issues in the Presbyterian church because the privy was directly above the church.

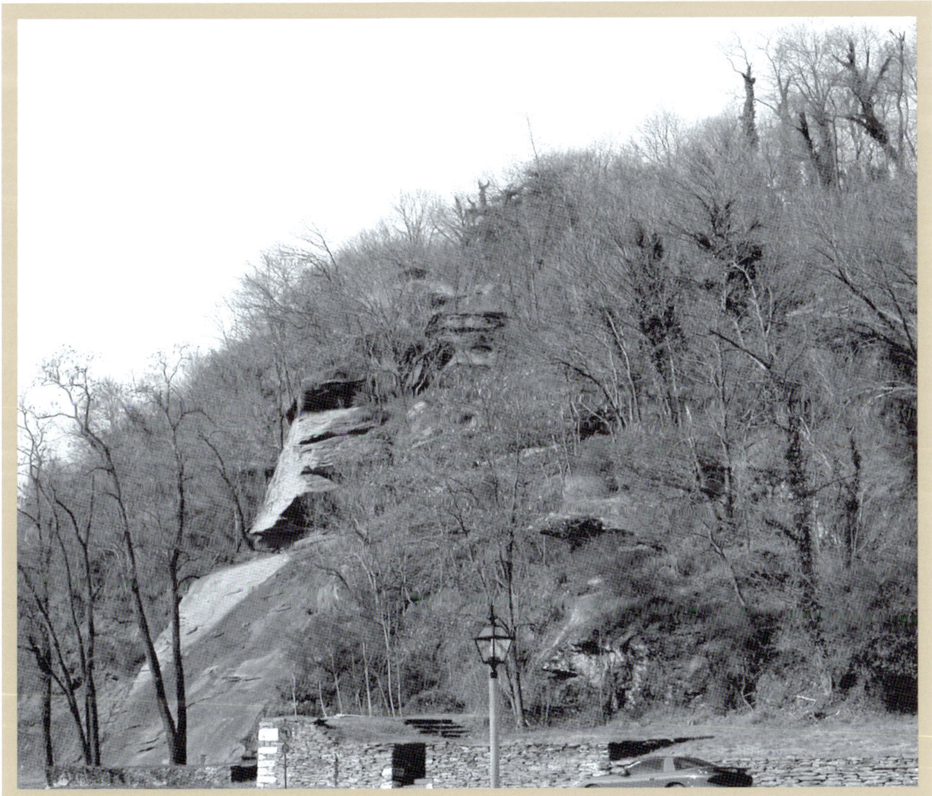

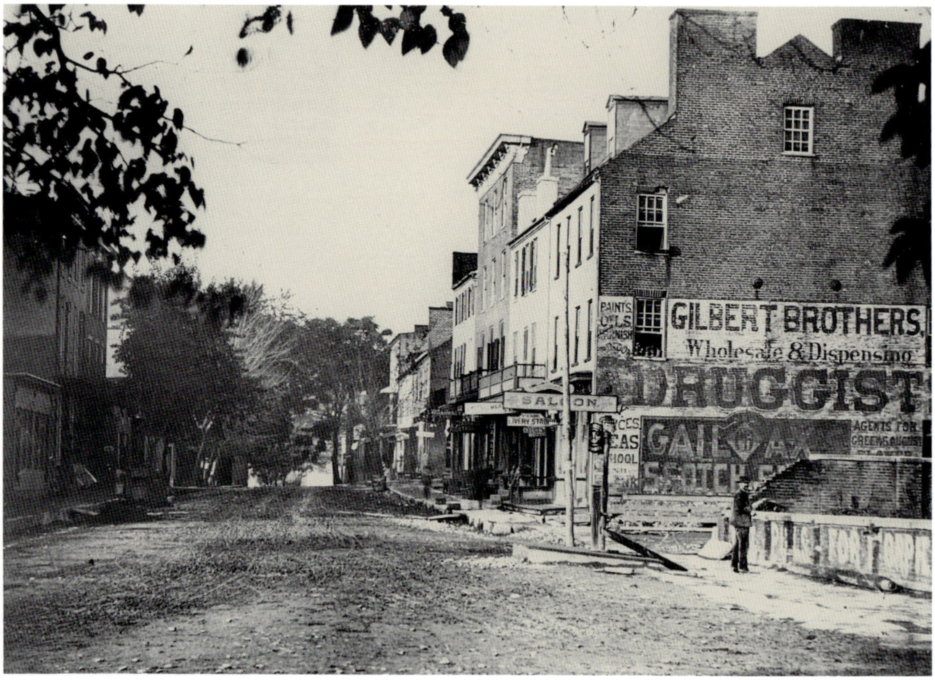

Today's view of this street looks very different from the photograph taken in 1890. This was the heart of the commercial district of yore. Today it is the heart of the historic district, claiming fame as home of the majority of the park's historical exhibits. No parking is allowed along Shenandoah Street today. All tourists must either park at Cavalier Heights Visitor Center and take a shuttle bus into town or park in the limited parking along Potomac Street. At the time of the old photograph, there were many buildings on the left side of the street that would later be razed by the park service.

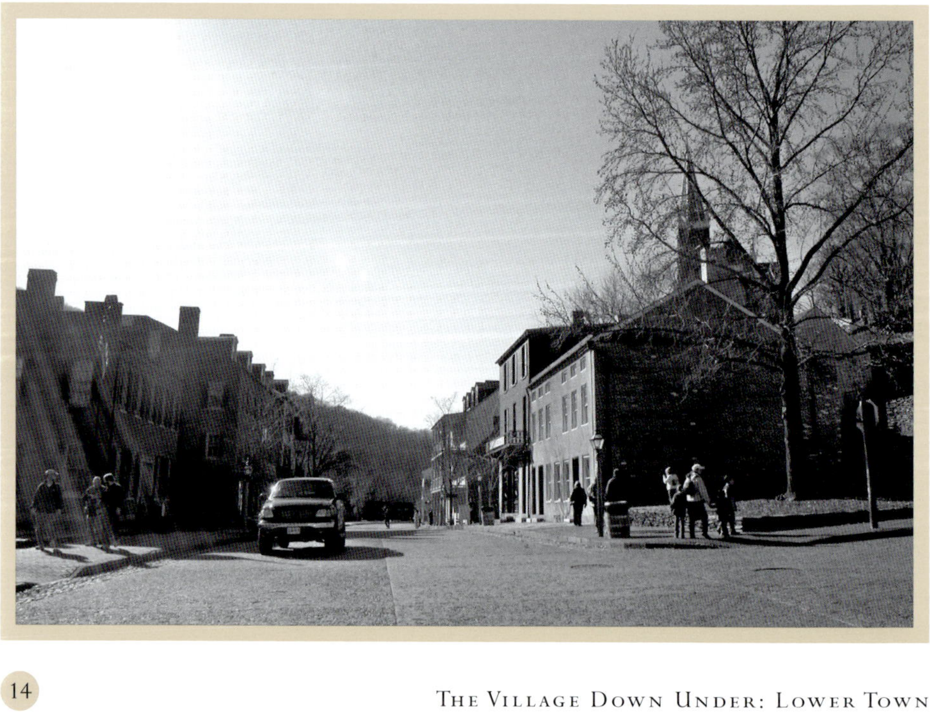

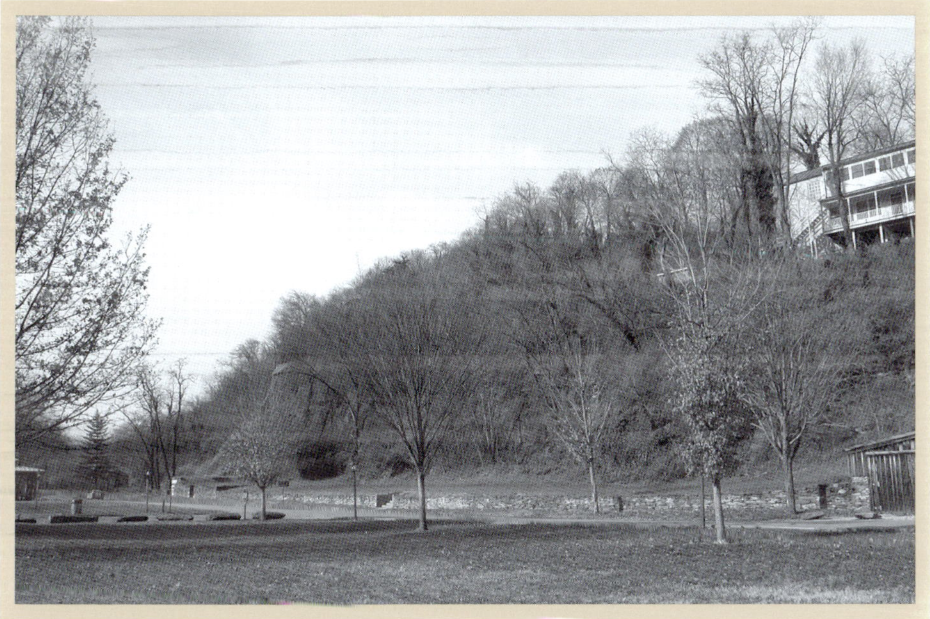

Today the lot where the former jail was located is barren of a building. The stone jail was torn down around 1950 by order of the Harpers Ferry Town Council. Reportedly, the stone was later recycled and used in the construction of a home on Ridge Street. A group of children sitting on a bench can be seen in front of the jail in the "then" photograph. Hopefully they were not waiting to get in.

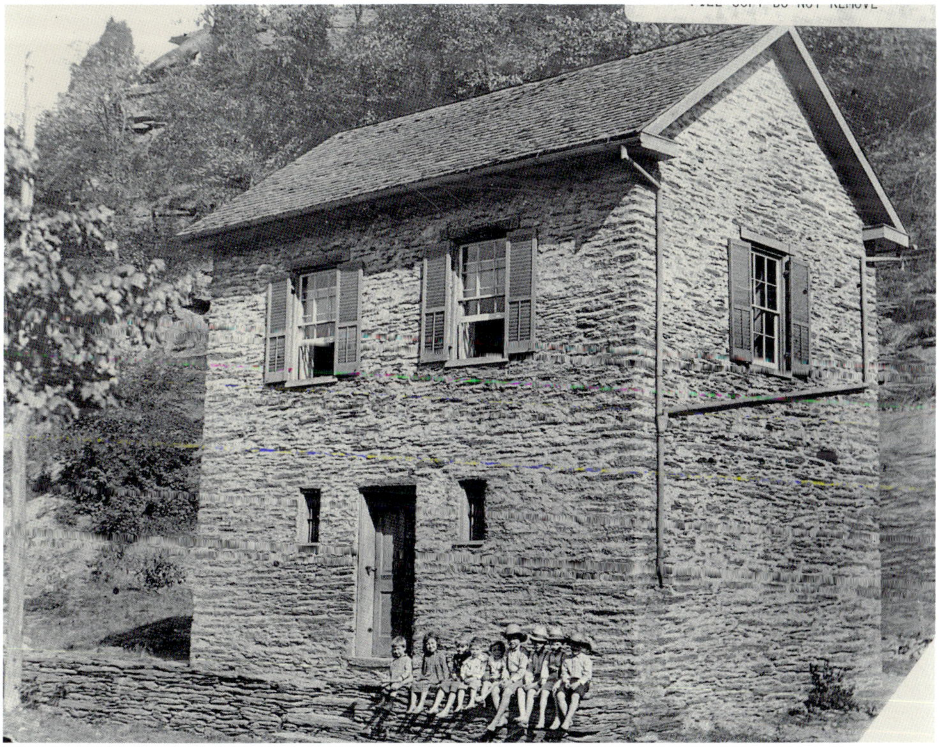

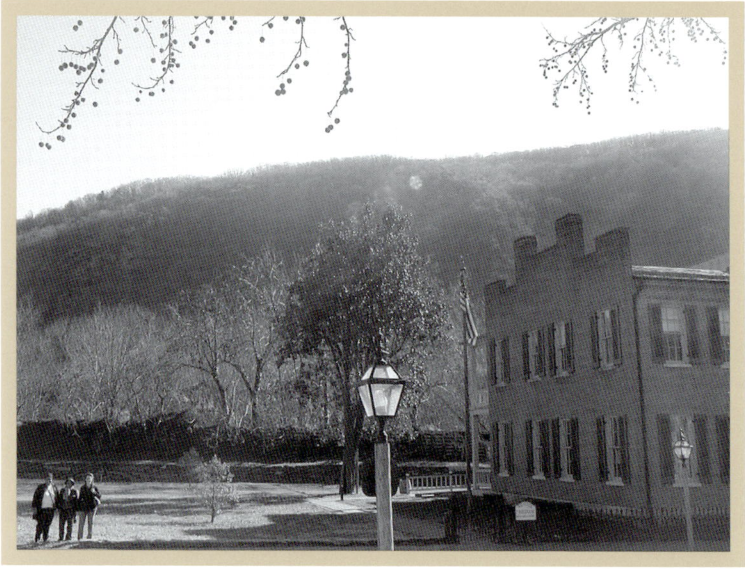

Lush and carefully manicured grass fills the space left by the building that was formerly on this spot. Known as Building No. 26, the brick building housed commercial ventures. Standing on the lot in the "now" photograph are, from left to right, as follows: Vivian McCathen from Montgomery Village in Gaithersburg, Maryland; Willia Dent from Suitland, Maryland; and Myra Burton from Bowie, Maryland. In the old photograph, the building to the right is the Master Armorer's House, which still exists today and serves as an exhibit center for the park.

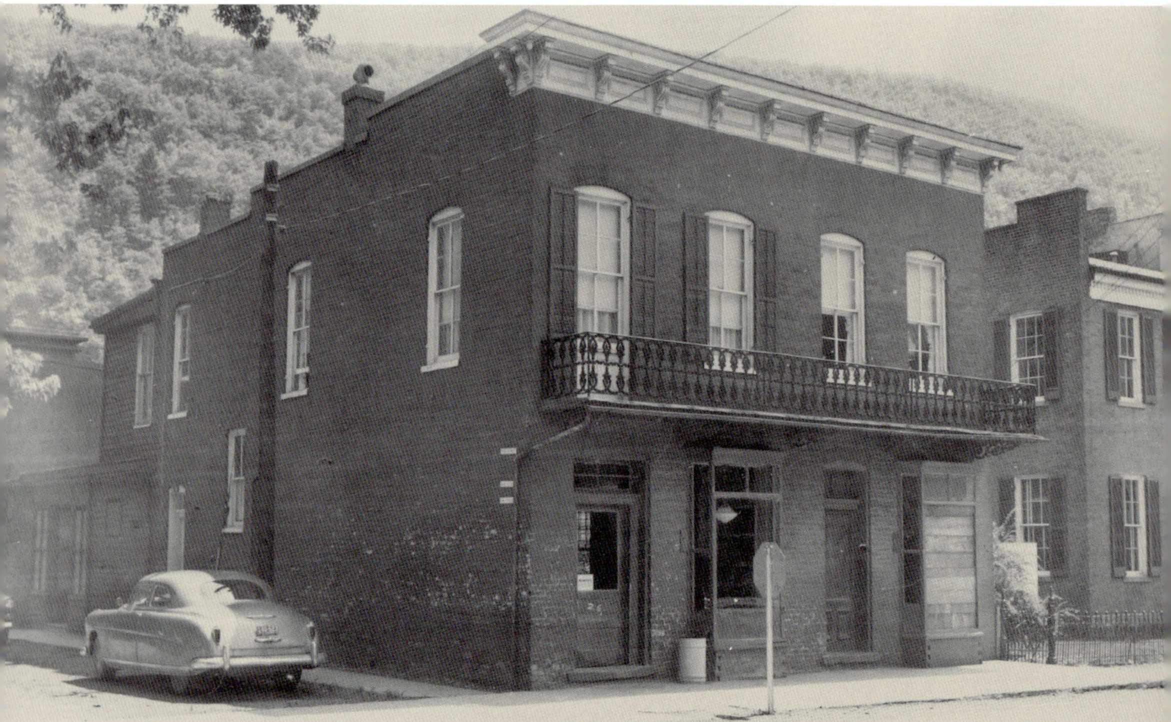

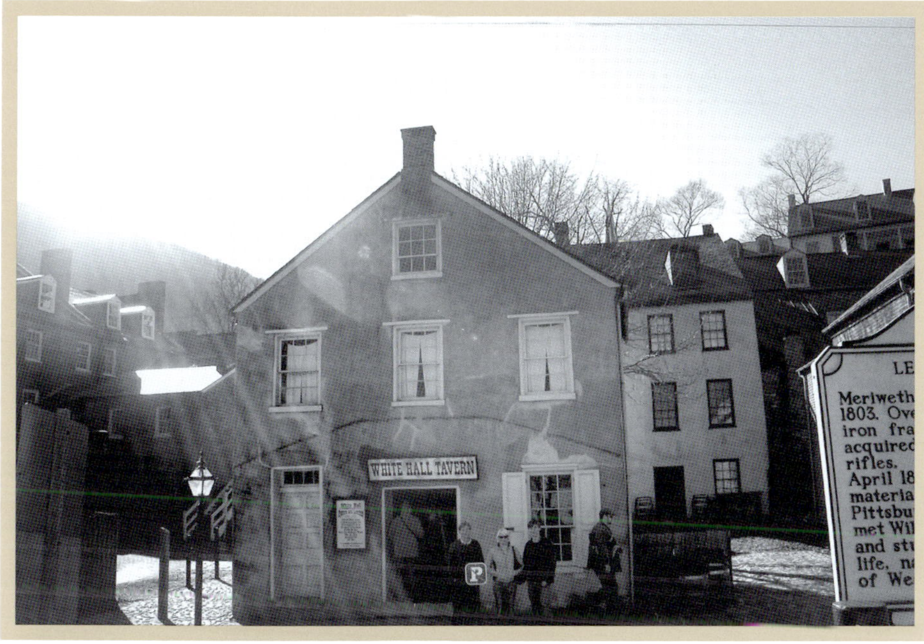

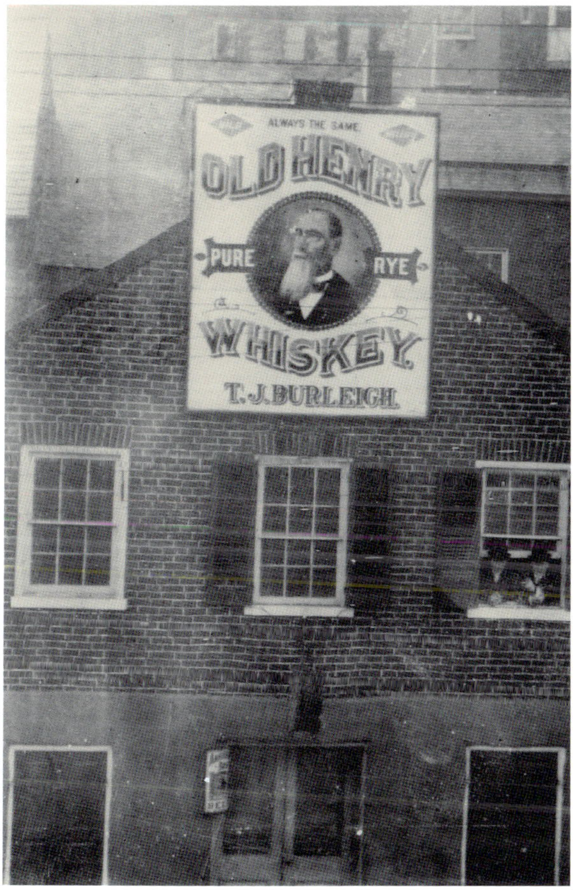

The "then" photograph of Building No. 5 was taken in the early 1900s. It shows the building being used as a beer tavern operated by T. J. Burleigh. The sign in the old photograph advertises "Old Henry / Pure Rye / Whiskey / T. J. Burleigh." Two men can be seen in the upper right window. Standing in front of the building today are, from left to right, the following: Blaine Gibson from Seattle, Washington; Suzi Slomack from Chicopee, Massachusetts; and Vladimir Gololobov from Siberia. All three live in Washington, D.C. Today the building houses the Lewis and Clark Exhibit on Potomac Street.

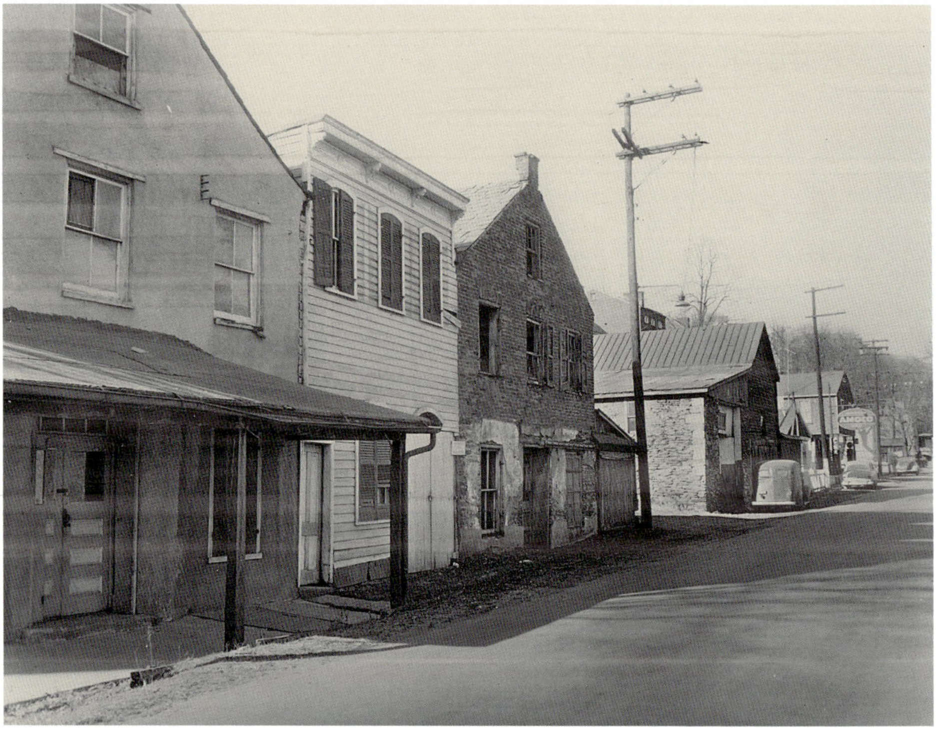

Named Potomac Street after the river along which it winds, today the street has buildings with a variety of uses. Some are historical exhibits and some are commercial ventures. In addition, farther down the street on the right are the train station and its parking lot. In the past, many more buildings were located here. There is limited two-hour parking along the street, but visitors are encouraged to park at the Cavalier Heights Center.

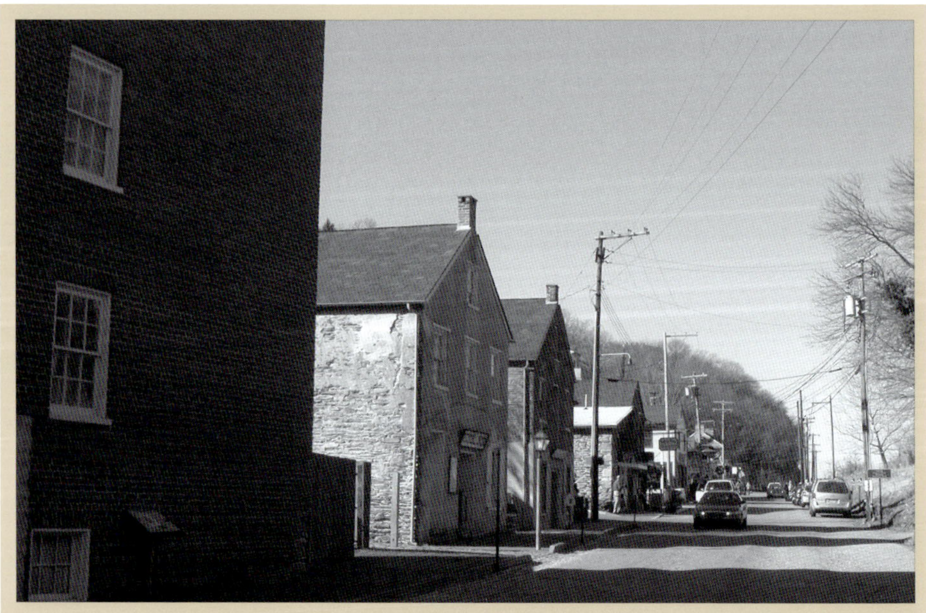

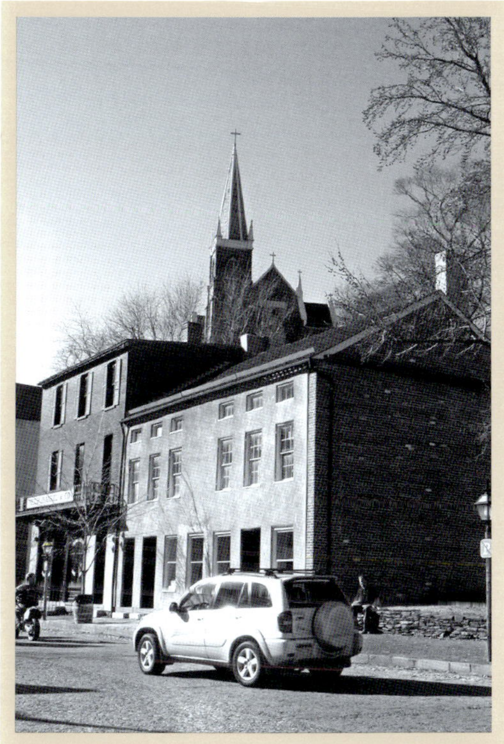

St. Peter's Catholic Church towers above Shenandoah Street in these Lower Town photographs. Pictured in the 1865 photograph are various buildings that today house the Archeology Exhibit, the Ready-Made Clothing Exhibit, and the Industry Exhibit. While the 1865 photograph shows the buildings with Civil War damage, today the buildings have been pristinely restored. The Ready-Made Clothing Exhibit is located in the William Richards Building, which was built in 1824.

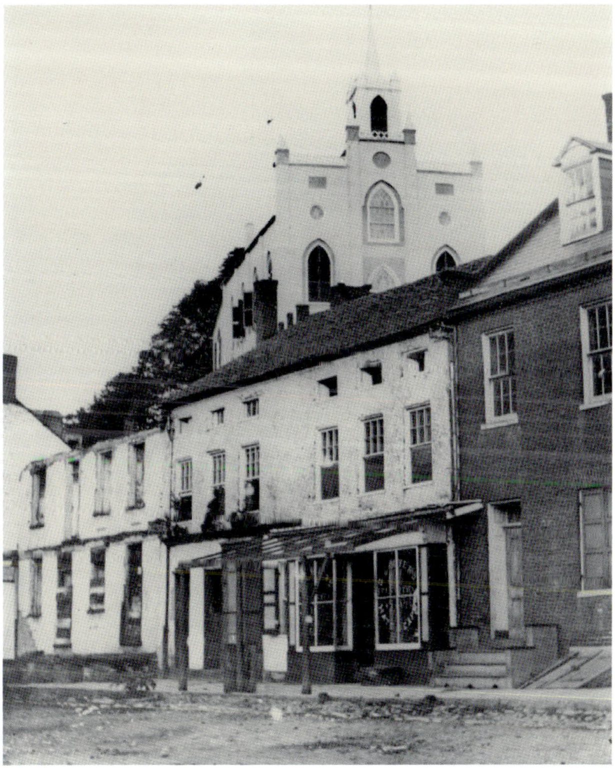

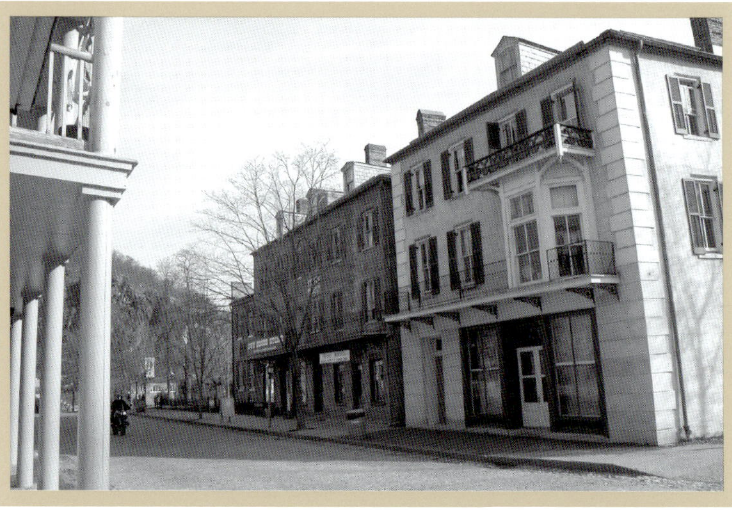

Lower Town has boasted numerous businesses over the years. Today the buildings along Shenandoah Street are all park service buildings. In the past, a local hardware merchant, James McGraw, erected a building to house his enterprise in 1882. Today the park exhibit "Harpers Ferry: A Place in Time" is located in that building, on the corner of Shenandoah Street and the former Market Street.

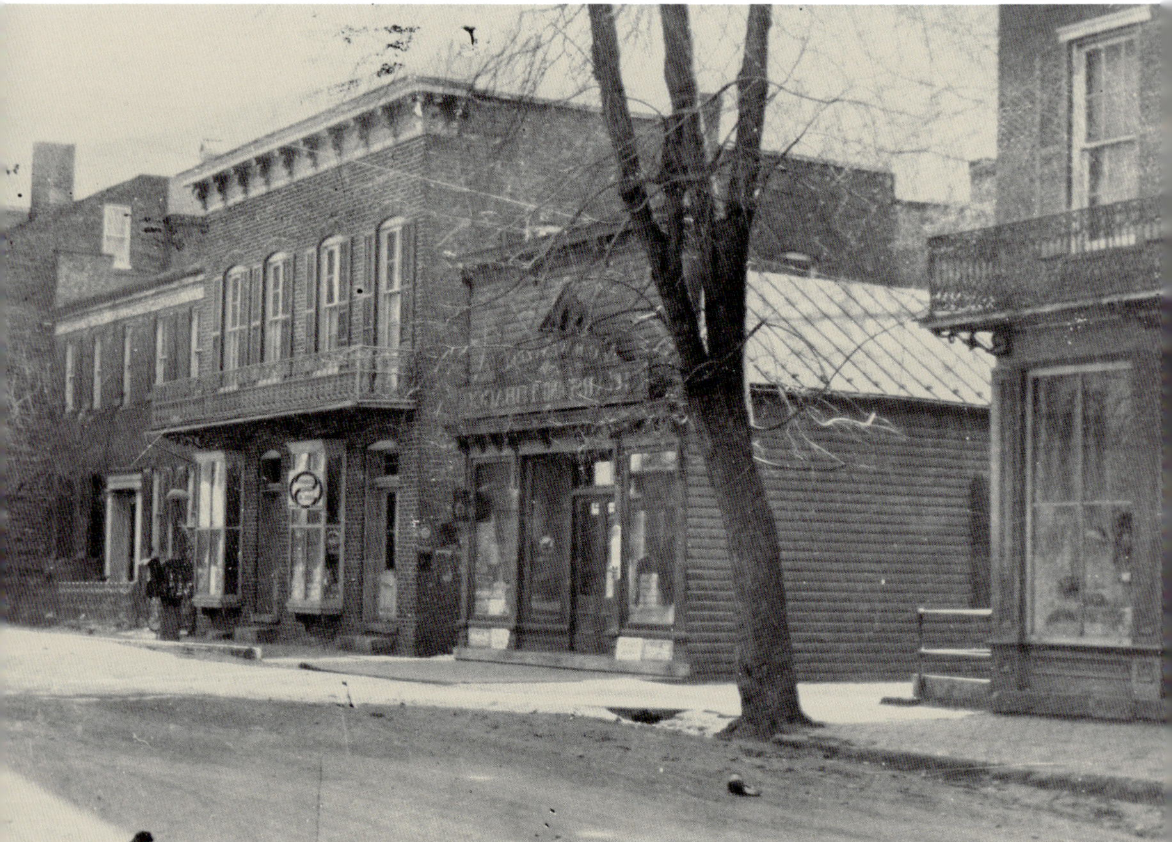

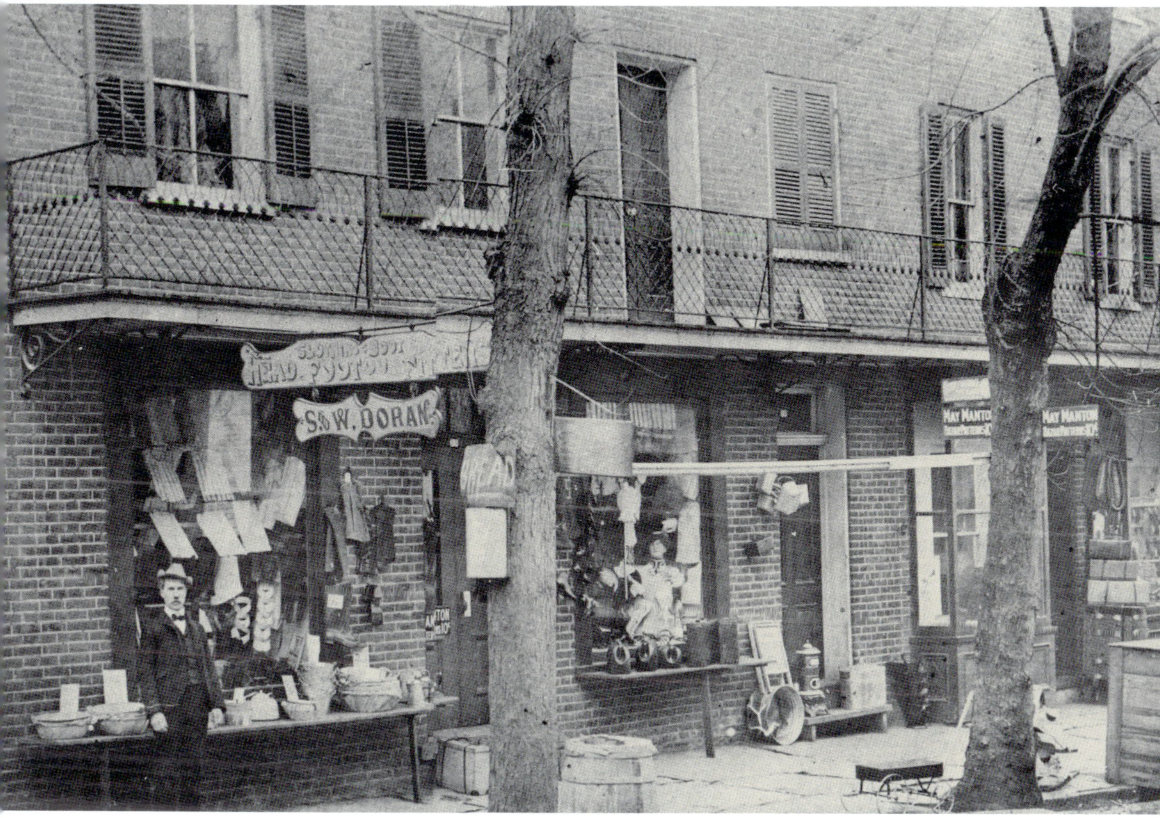

The Provost Marshall's Office and the Old Master Armorer's Quarters are located where these stores were located in days gone by. The office is a replica of the headquarters of the military commander of the town during the Civil War. From the looks of the photograph from the late 1890s, a Mr. Doran had a successful store on the south side of Shenandoah Street.

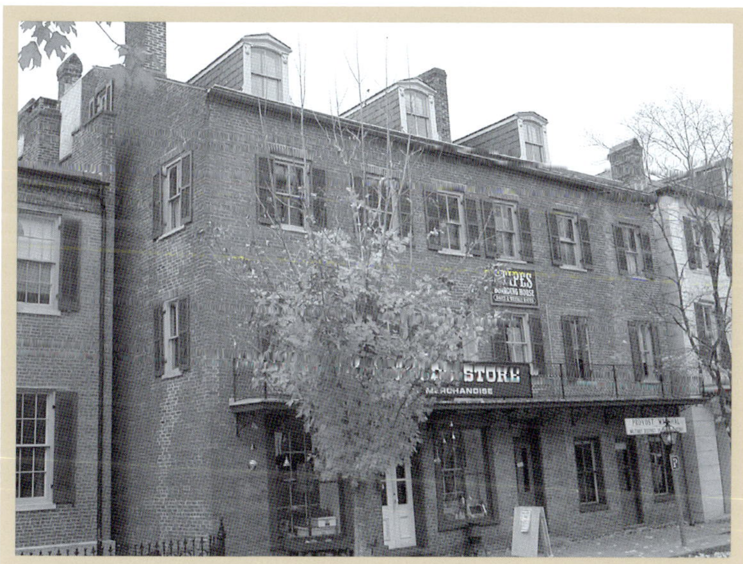

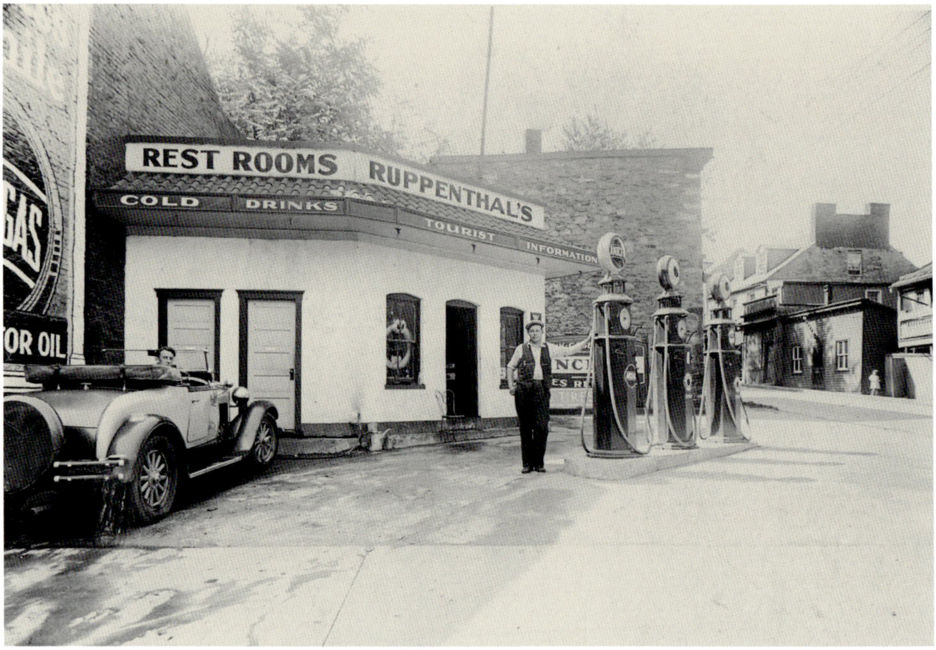

The corner of High Street and Shenandoah Streets has seen many changes over the years. Today it is a neatly manicured little respite for weary hikers to rest after they descend the Stone Stairs. Visitors can rest either on the grass under the shade of the tree or sit on the edge of the stone wall. In days of yore, it was an Amoco gas station, as this *c.* 1930 photograph shows.

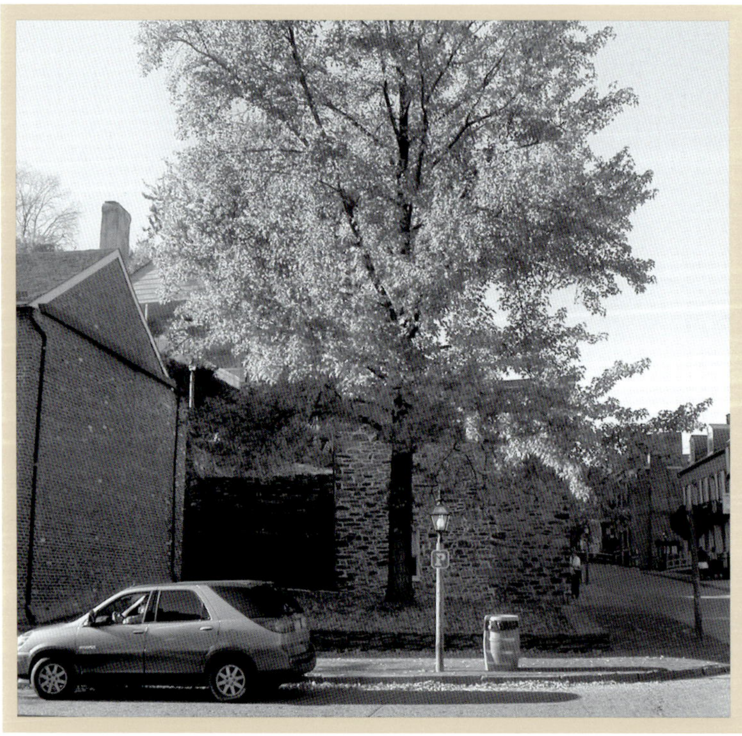

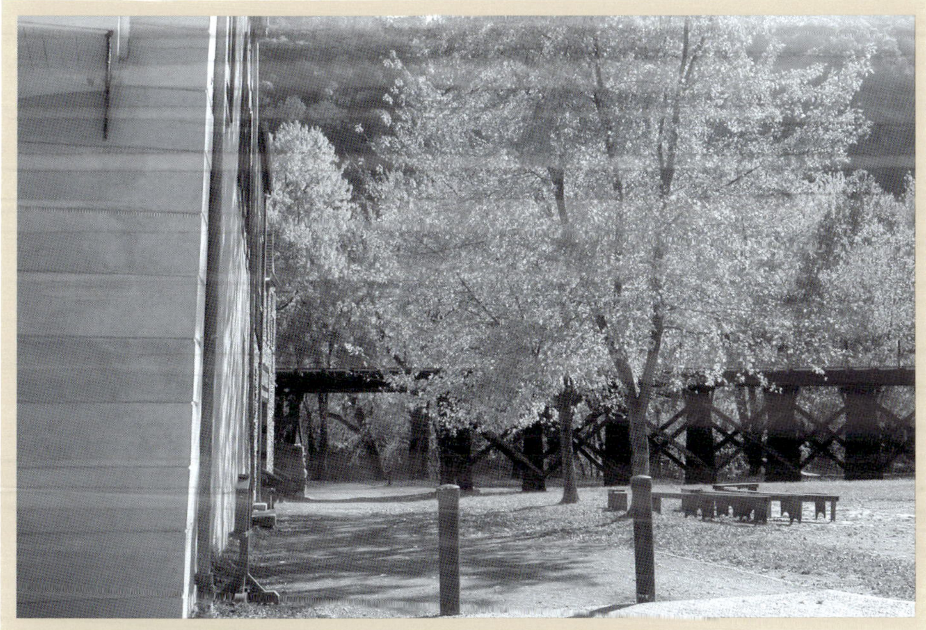

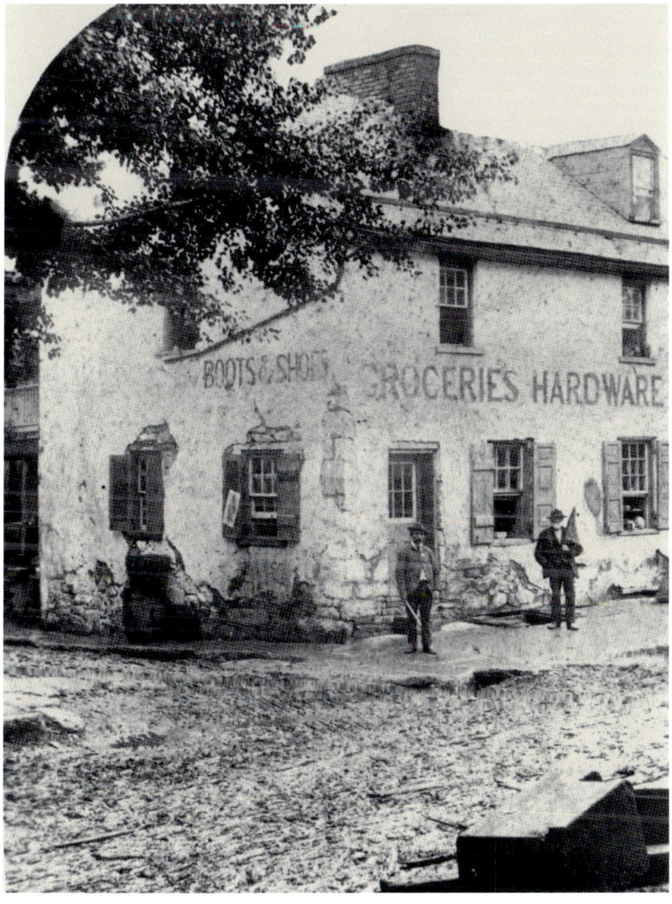

The corner of Shenandoah and Market Streets today is vacant except for an area where park rangers give their talks, with benches provided for the visitors. Prior to the flood of 1889, there was a grocery and hardware store here, which also offered boots and shoes for sale. On Shenandoah Street alone, there are approximately 23 locations where buildings no longer exist, destroyed by either man or Mother Nature.

On the north side of Shenandoah Street, the first building on the left of this photograph is the Old Stage Coach Inn, which today houses the bookstore for the Harpers Ferry Historical Association. Next to it is the building that houses restrooms for visitors, and then comes the building that houses the Industrial Museum. The old photograph was taken between 1882 and 1889 and shows what appear to be several prospering businesses.

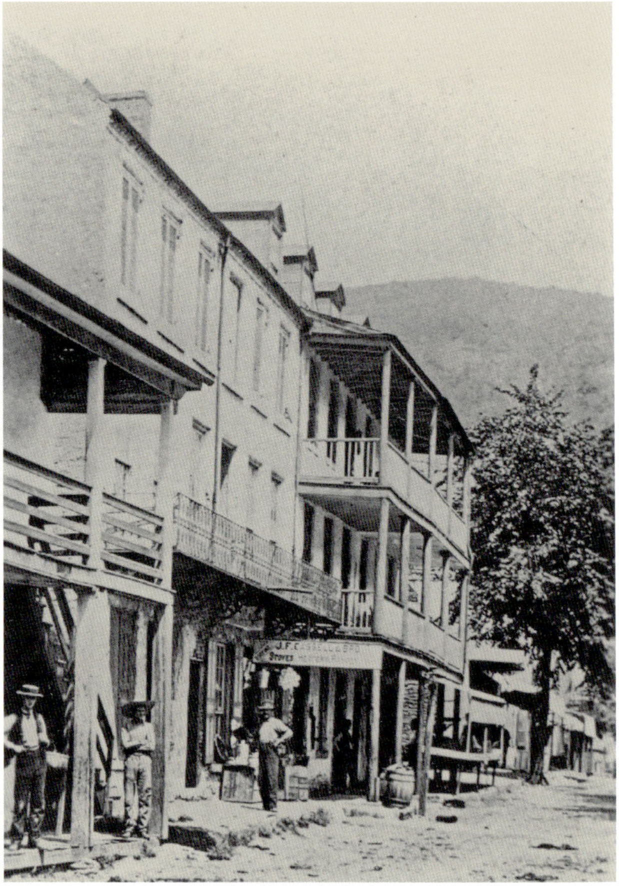

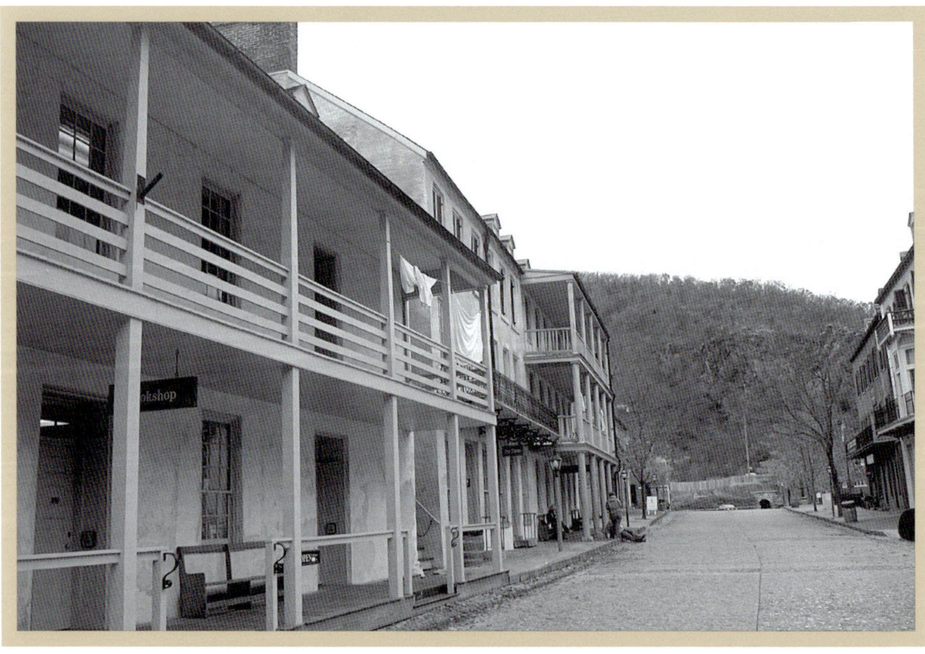

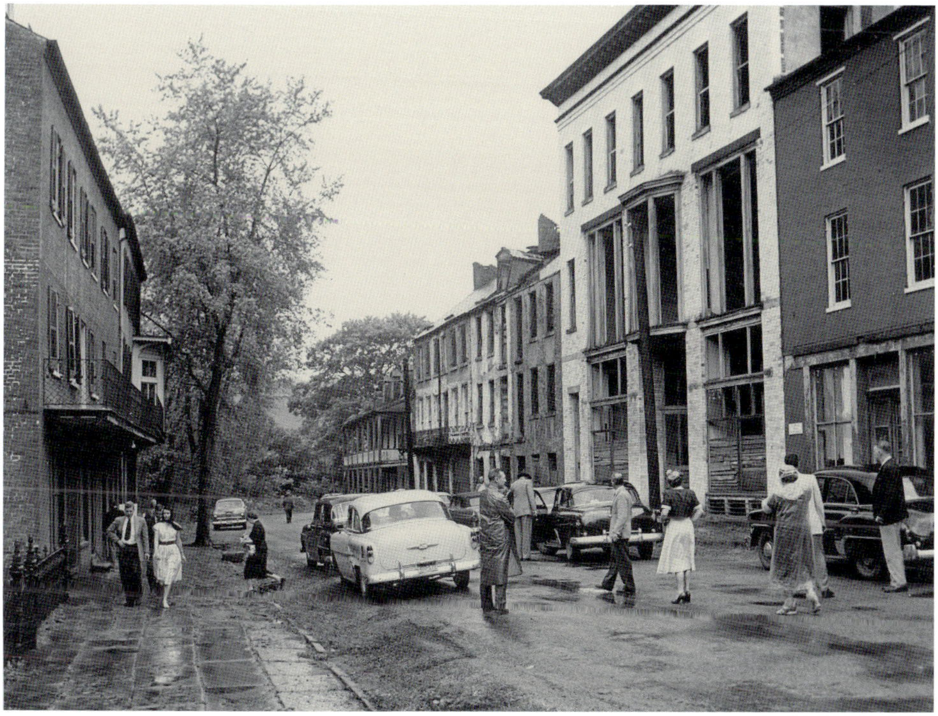

Pristinely restored park buildings line the north side of Shenandoah Street. In the past, all were prosperous commercial ventures, most with living quarters above. The old photograph was taken around 1955 and shows cars parked along the street, something that is not allowed today. In addition, very little of the restoration of the buildings had begun. With the restoration completed, the town appears today very much as it did in 1859.

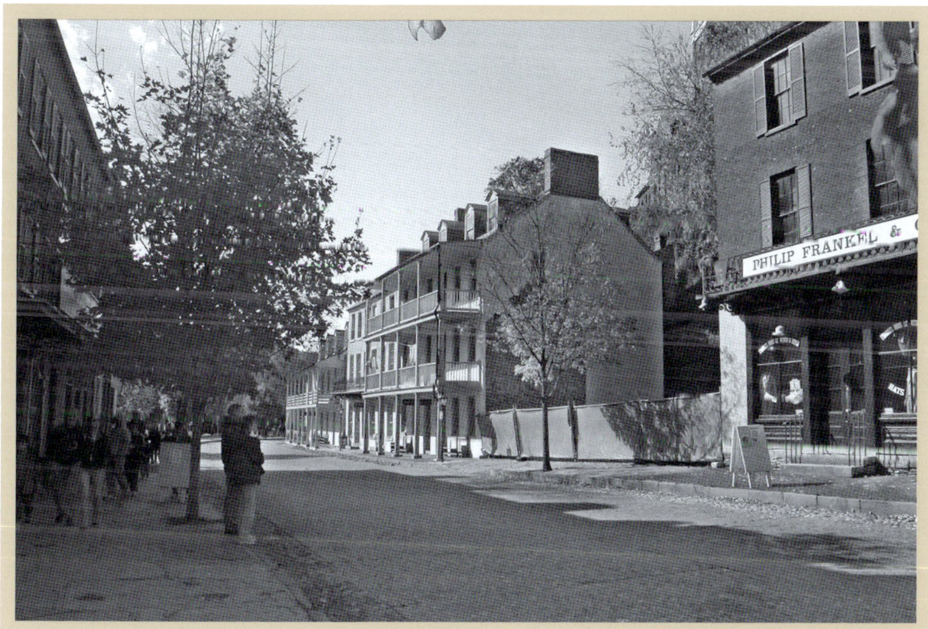

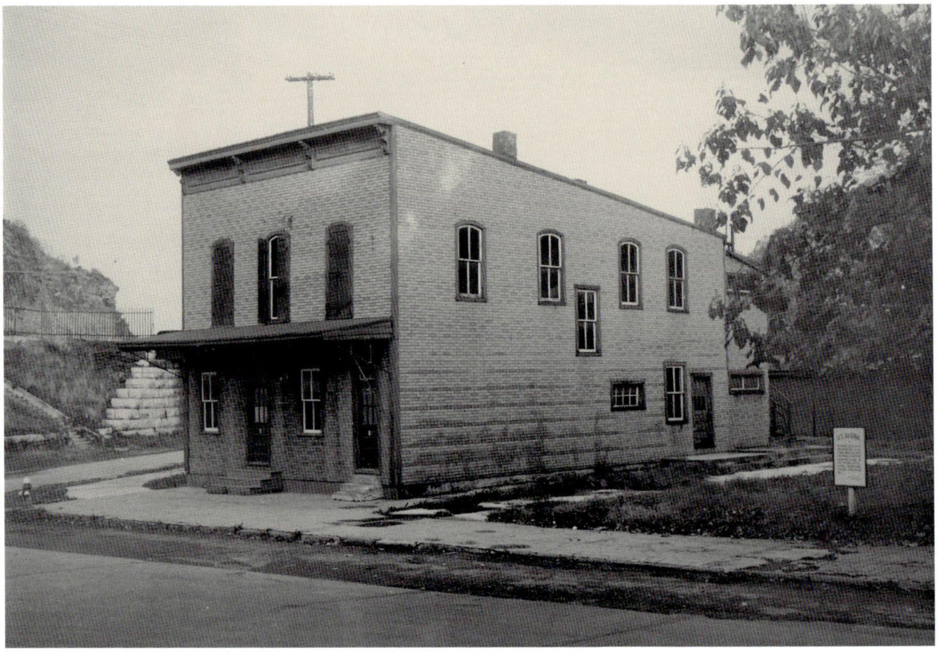

Today the Harpers Ferry Post Office is located in the Upper Town on Washington Street. In days gone by, it was located in the Lower Town on Shenandoah Street across the street from the train station, which was then located at the end of the street. This area was known as Arsenal Square, where the large arsenal was located. During John Brown's raid, many of the guns that had been stored in the arsenal had been moved to the Upper Town because of the danger that floods posed. Pictured here are, from left to right, tourists Mary and Howard Wallace from Bellevue, Ohio, and their son, Patrick Wallace, from Funkstown, Maryland.

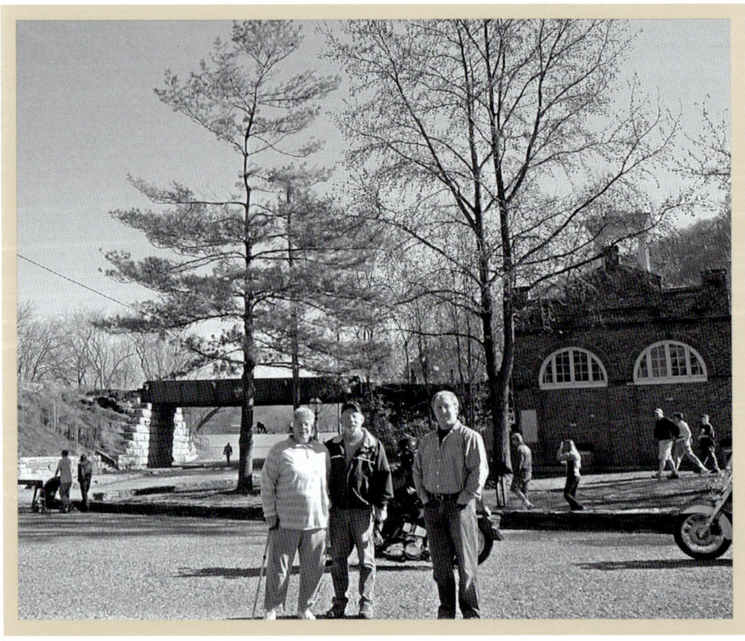

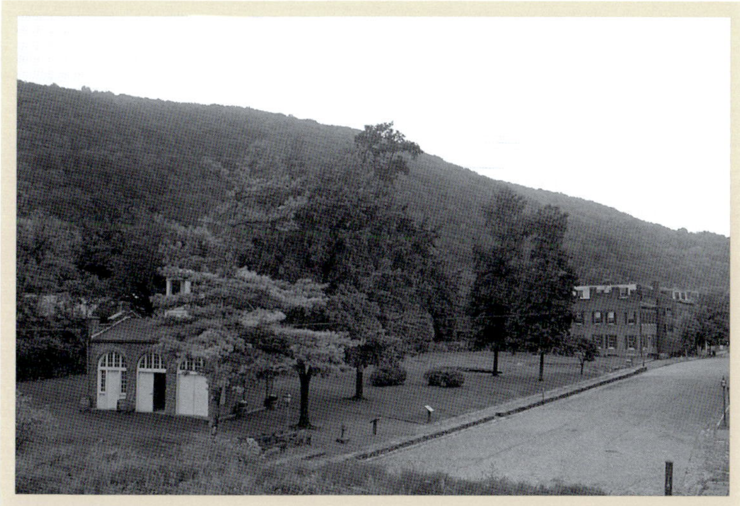

John Brown's Fort is prominently displayed today on the area that used be the home of the Connor Hotel. The grassy area visible in the "now" photograph was filled with buildings in years gone by. The Connor Hotel offered both room and meals. It was equipped with electric lights, electric call bells, and hot and cold baths, something not all hotels offered. The hotel was located on the original site of the U.S. Arsenal.

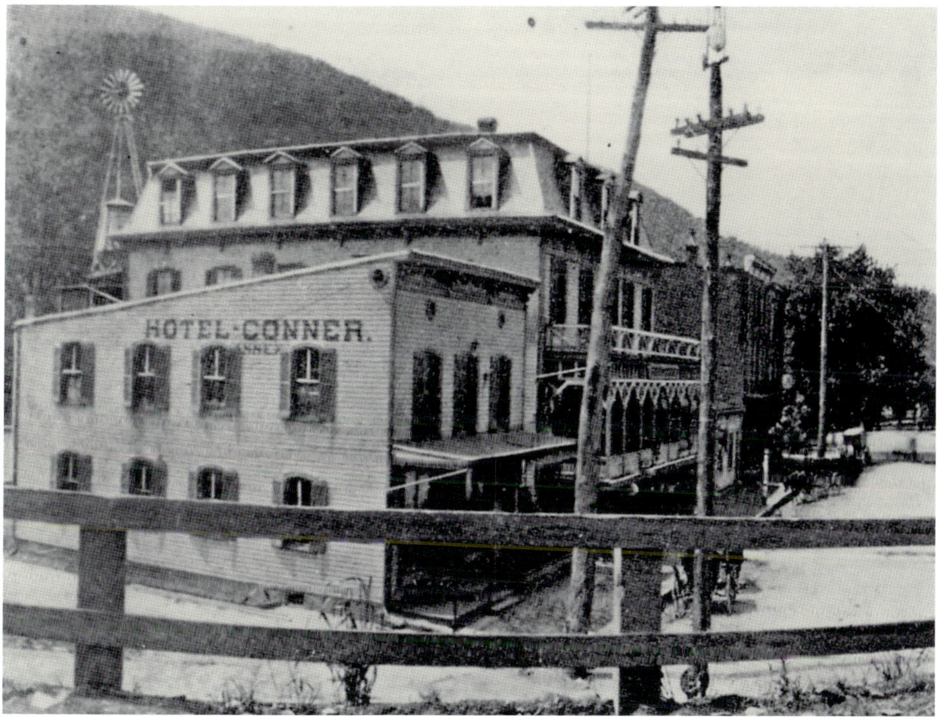

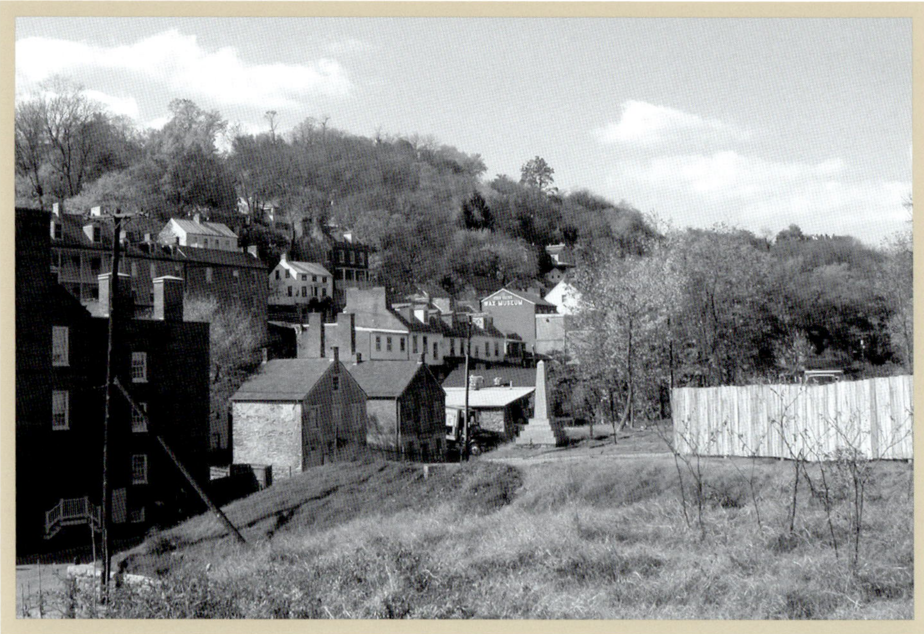

It is difficult to visualize what this area was like in 1859. Although the fort is no longer in its original location, we can imagine it sitting on the spot where the obelisk now stands. The brick, three-story Gerard Bond Wager building is visible on the left in each photograph. It was constructed between 1837 and 1838. Gerard Bond Wager was a second-generation heir to the town's founder, Richard Harper.

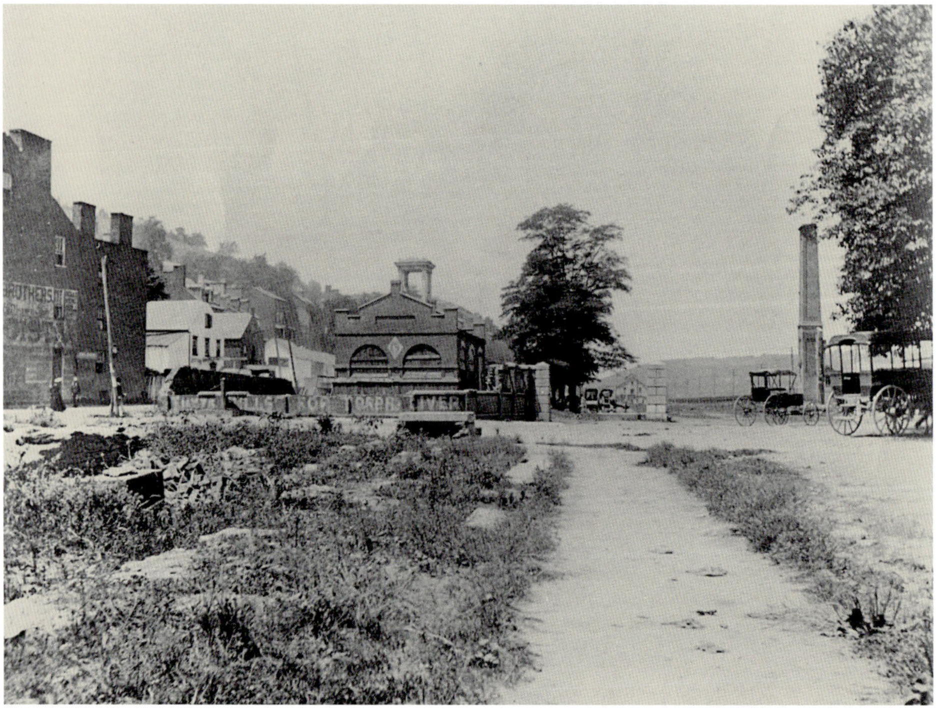

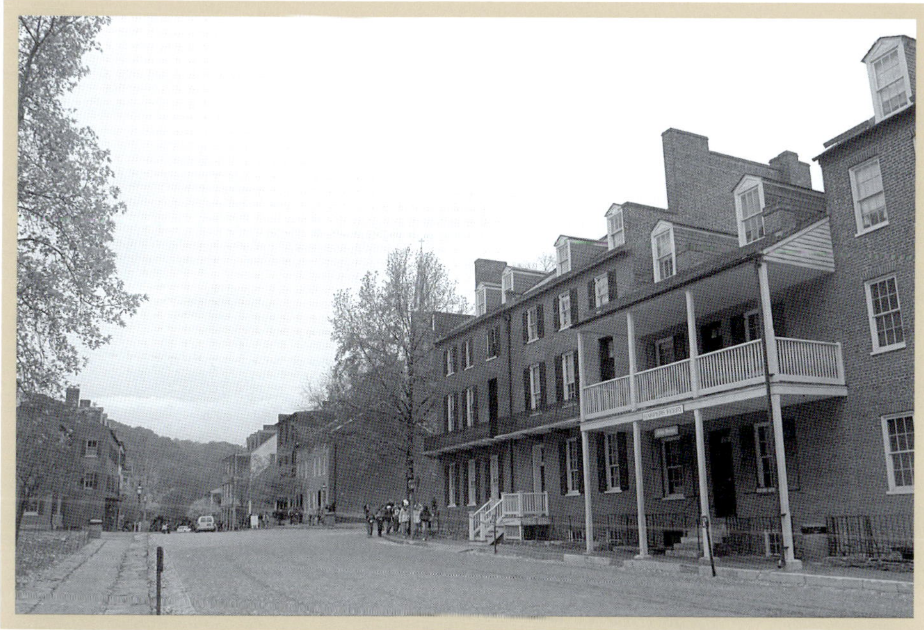

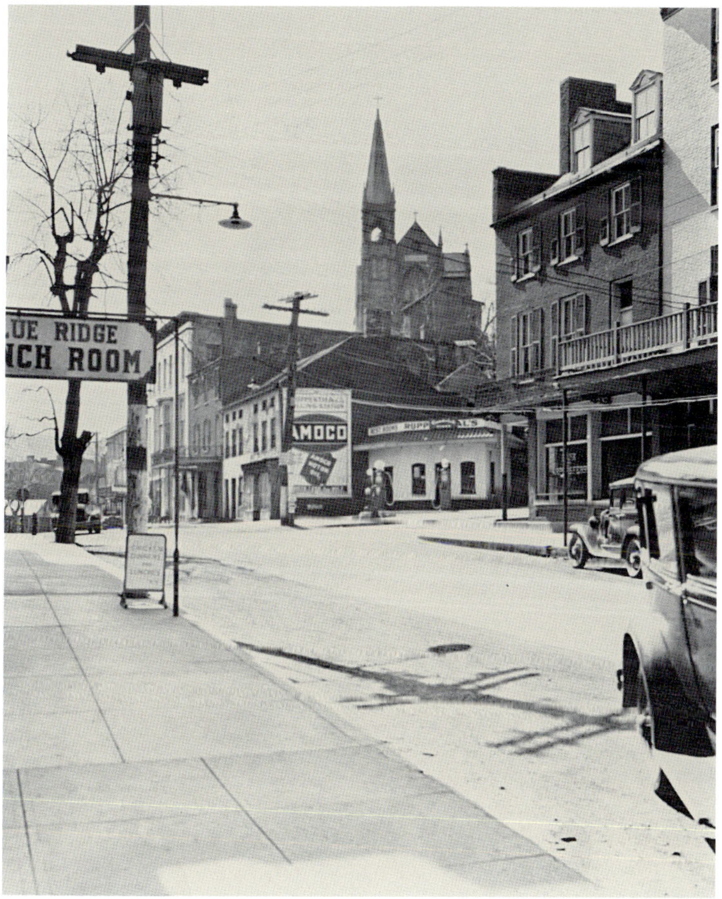

This comprehensive photograph shows many buildings that have been restored by the National Park Service on the north side of Shenandoah Street. The group of tourists is standing in front of the Ann C. Stephenson Building, which in years past housed the Harpers Ferry Hotel. Today it houses a park exhibit. Just beyond the group is the Tearney Building, which also houses an exhibit. The Tearney Building is adjacent to the vacant lot where the Amoco Station was formerly located.

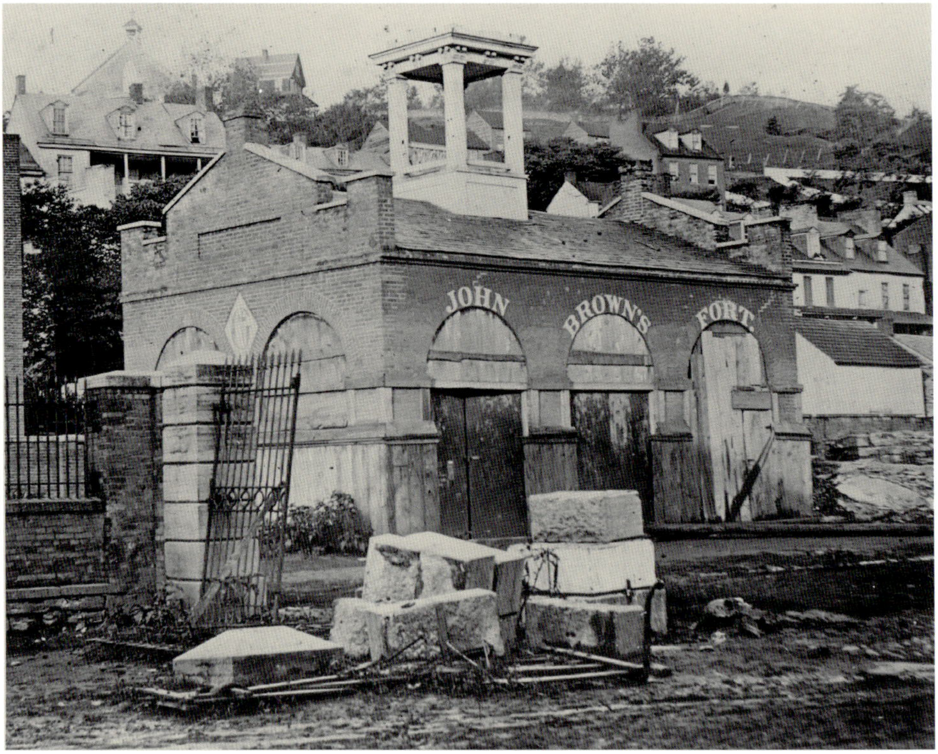

John Brown's Fort has been in several locations throughout its lifespan. In this *c.* 1890 photograph, it is located in the Lower Town on its original site. It was sold in 1891, removed, and in 1892 it went on display at the World's Columbian Exposition in Chicago, after which it was dismantled. In 1895, it was rebuilt on Alexander Murphy's farm. Storer College purchased it in 1903. In 1960, it was sold to the National Park Service and was moved to the Lower Town in 1968.

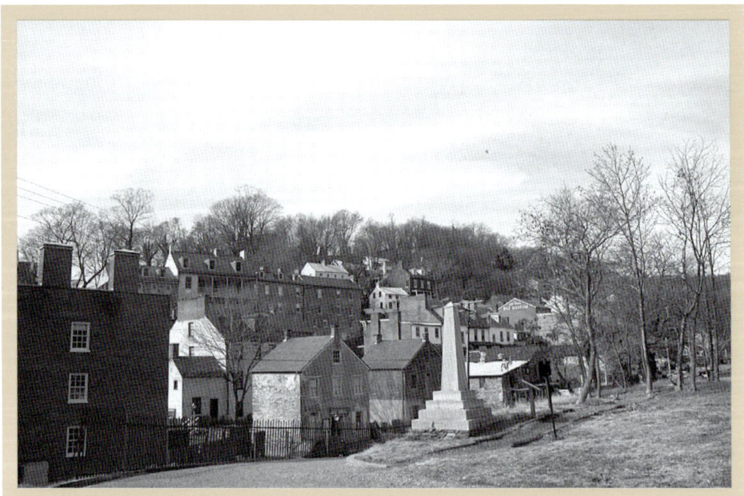

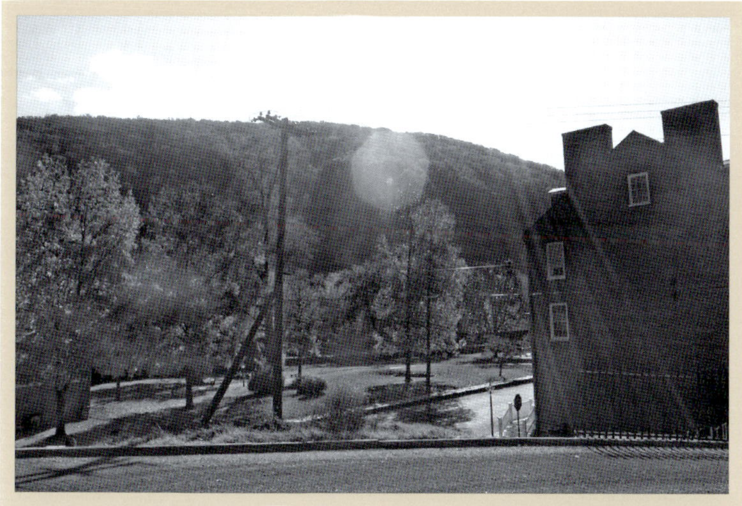

Gates to the Armory Yard dominate this *c.* 1859 photograph. It is speculated that the town's first settler, Peter Stephens, might have built his log cabin on the site of the Gerard Bond Wager building, which is the brick building seen on the right side of both photographs. In 1860, nineteen lots in the Lower Town were owned by Gerard and his brother-in-law, Noah Swayne.

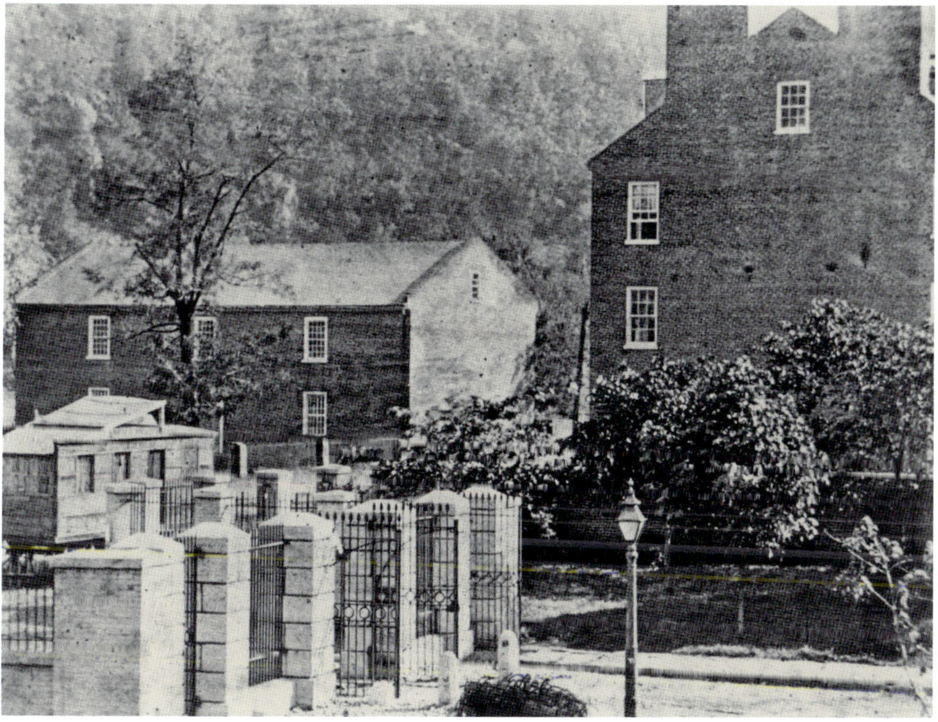

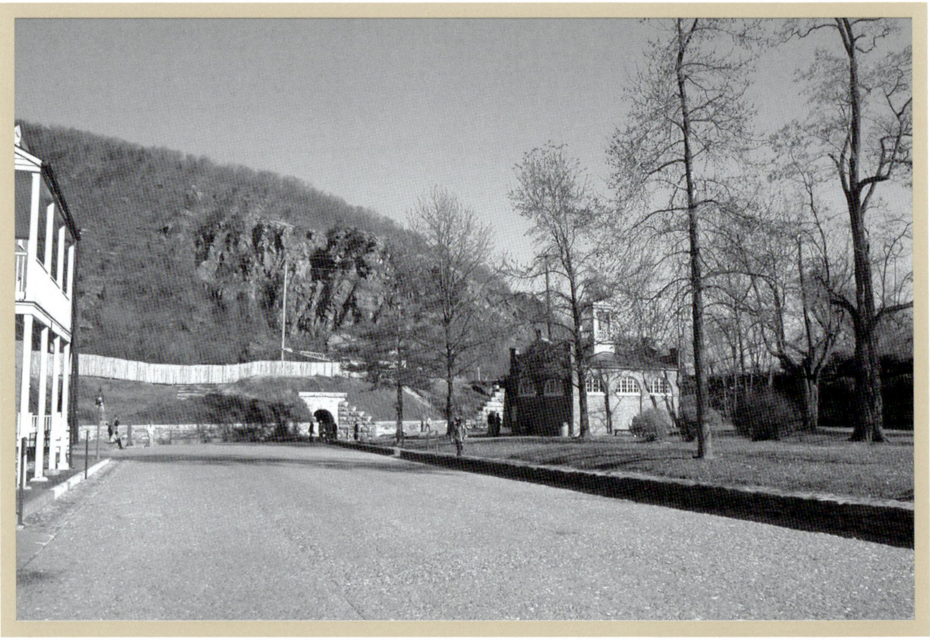

The Connor Hotel and the old post office are visible in this photograph from the 1930s. Today the area is well-manicured and maintained by the National Park Service, devoid of buildings with the exception of John Brown's Fort. This area is called Arsenal Square and was the home of the Large Arsenal, Small Arsenal, and the Superintendent's Office. Tourists can be seen in the "now" photograph enjoying the cool, crisp autumn weather.

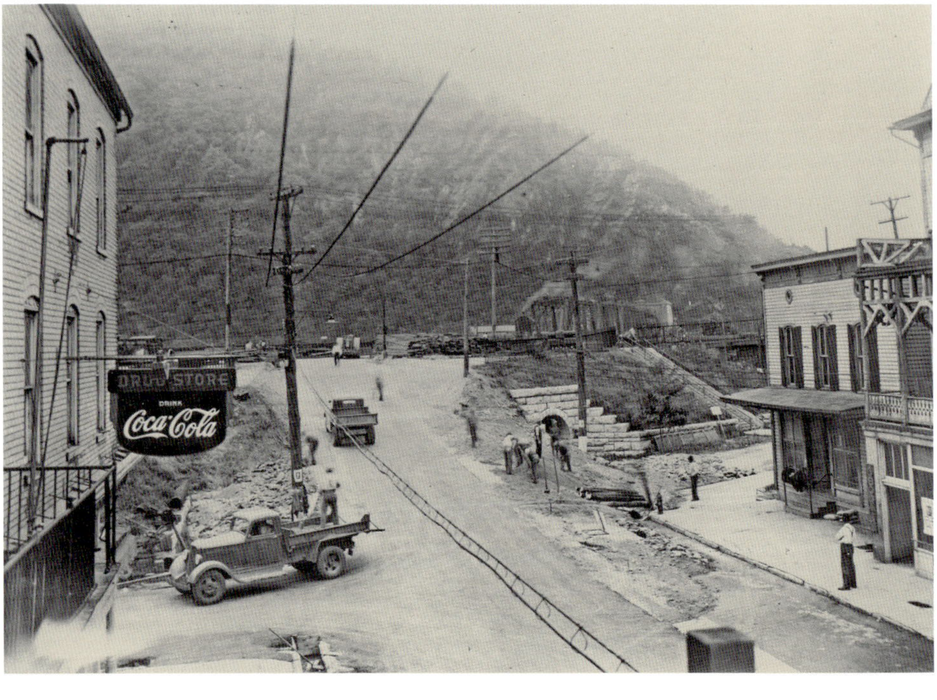

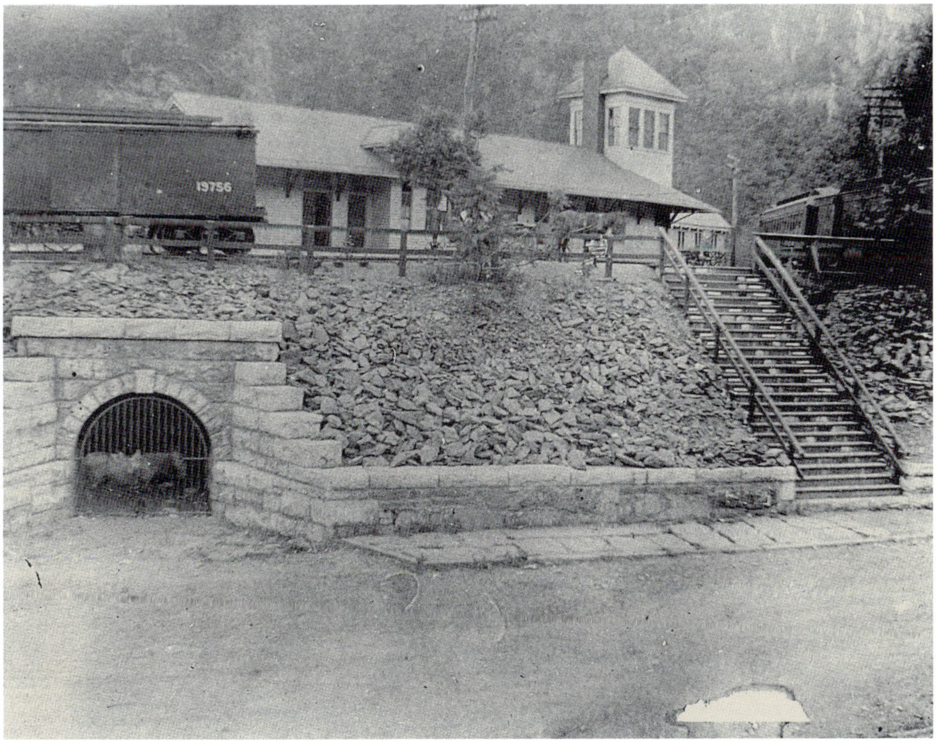

Pictured below is the railroad station prior to its removal to its new location. Today the stairs lead to a construction site, and pedestrians are not allowed. The Peterson family from Frederick, Maryland, can be seen just to the right of the entrance to the underpass. In the "then" photograph, a horse can be seen in the entrance to the underpass, which is a rare sight today. In the photograph on page 11, which begins this chapter, the train station is seen in the lower center of the photograph.

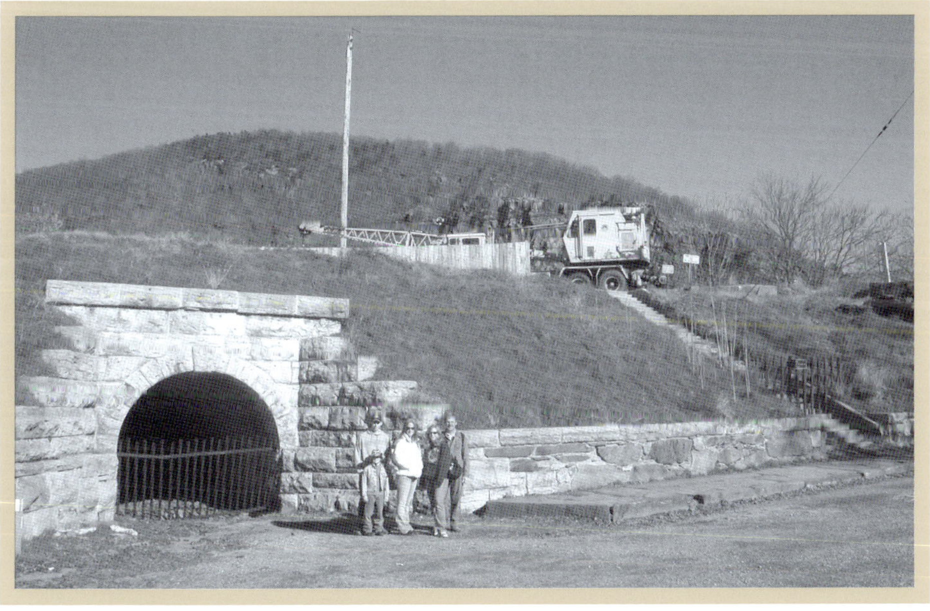

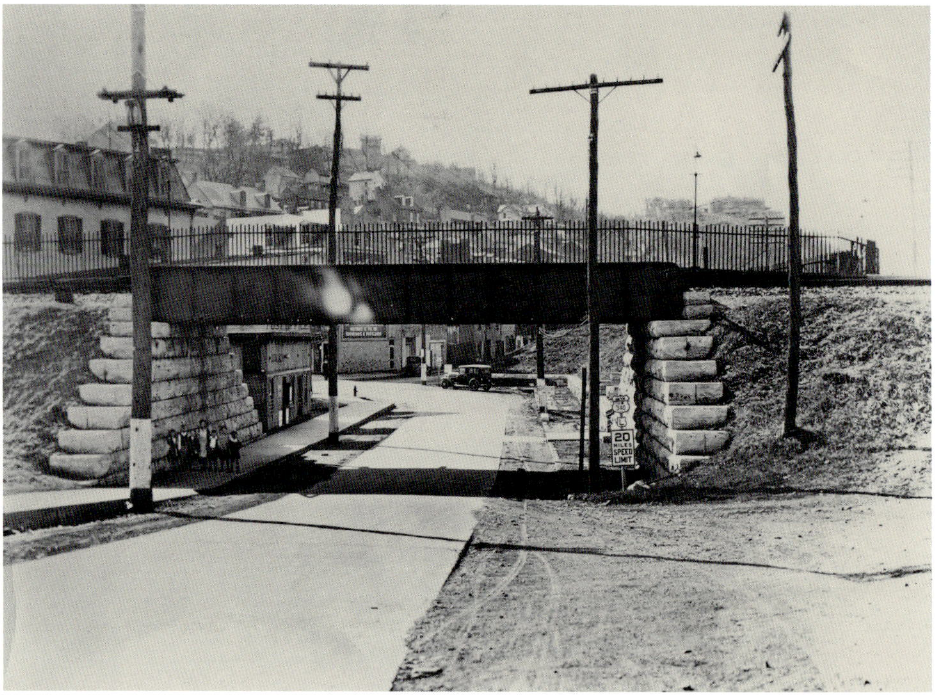

The road under this Winchester and Potomac Railroad overpass today is for foot traffic or maintenance vehicles only. Tourists are seen in the modern photograph having just walked through the underpass. The sign located on the right side of the old photograph says "340." Today Route 340 bypasses the downtown completely. The old post office was located on the left past the underpass. Farther along on 340, visible on the extreme left side of the photograph, is the old Connor Hotel.

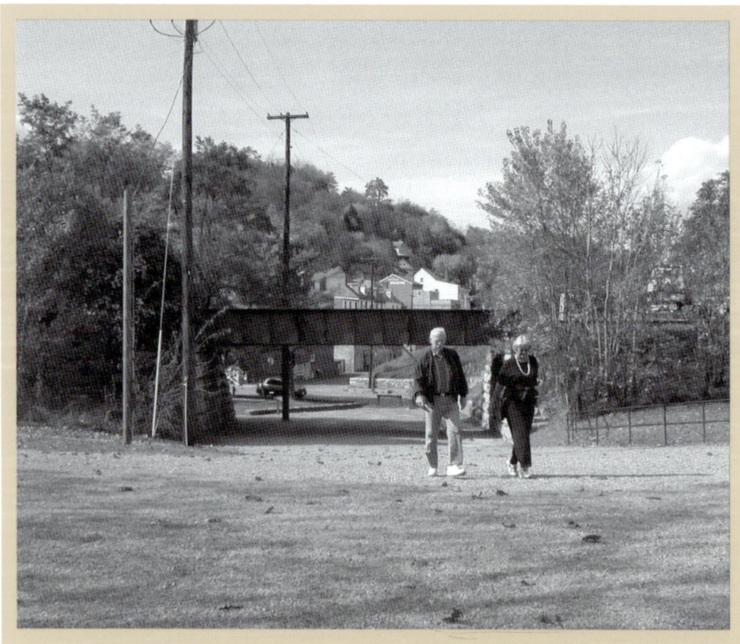

CHAPTER 2

Elevated Avenue

High Street

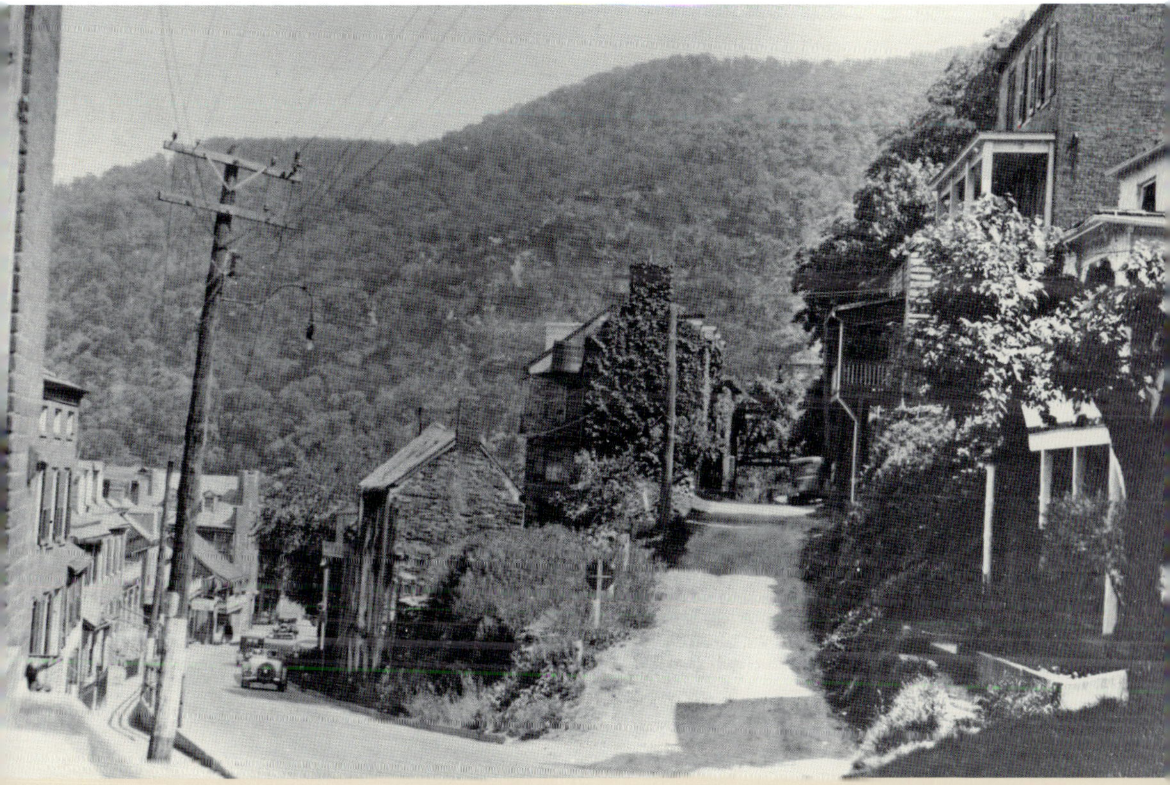

High Street serves as the on-ramp to the Upper Town. It meets Shenandoah Street in Lower Town, and as it extends farther up the hill, it intersects with Public Way and becomes Washington Street. Washington Street eventually meets Route 340 after approximately one and a half miles in a westerly direction. The distances are all small for this little town, but because of the hilly terrain, walking can be tiring.

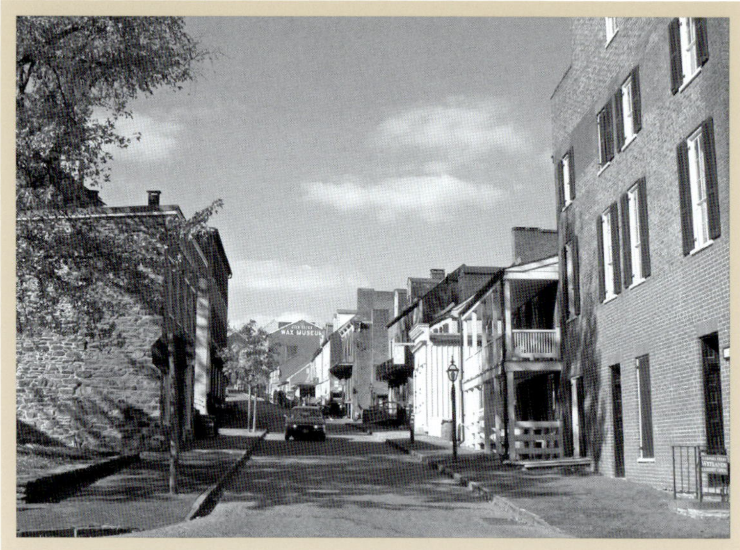

Although these photographs are deceiving, High Street is quite steep for walkers. Fortunately today there are railings higher up along the street to help pedestrians. John Brown's Wax Museum can be seen farther up the street on the right. Numerous quaint shops are available for shoppers. While cars do navigate the streets in Harpers Ferry, very little parking is allowed in the Lower Town. And a horse and buggy, as seen in the old photograph, are seldom seen.

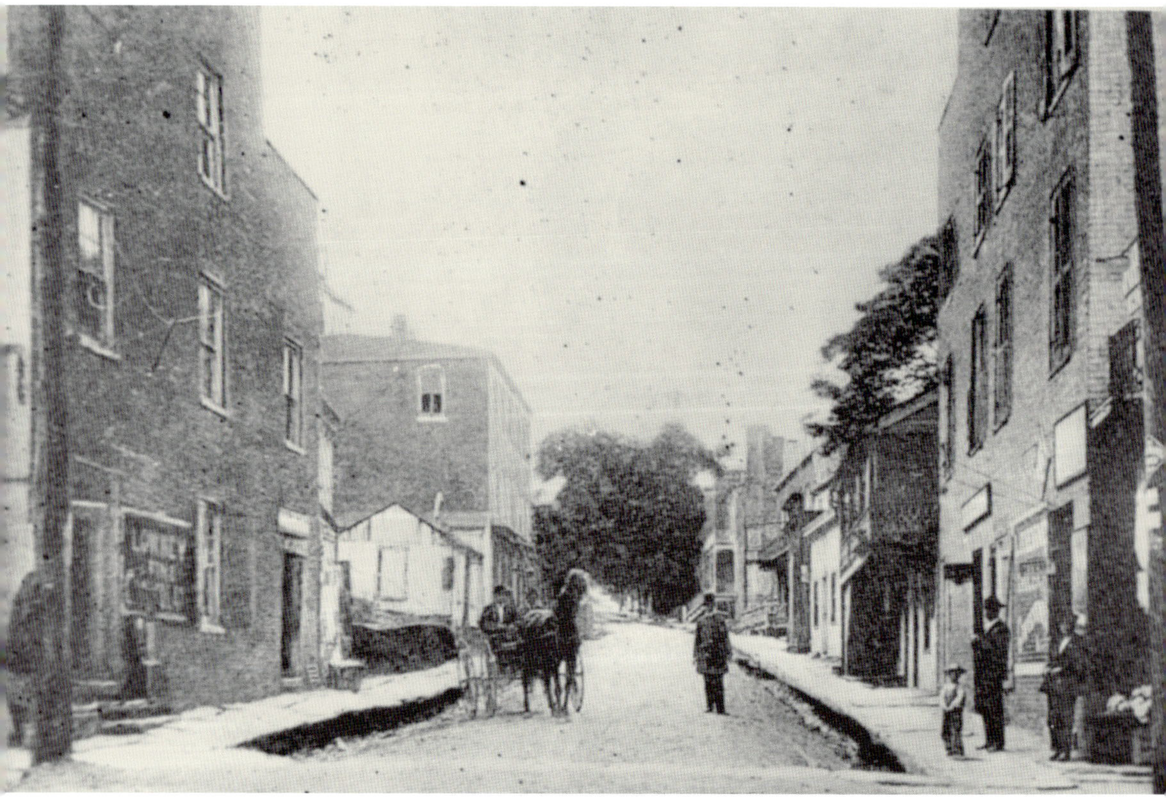

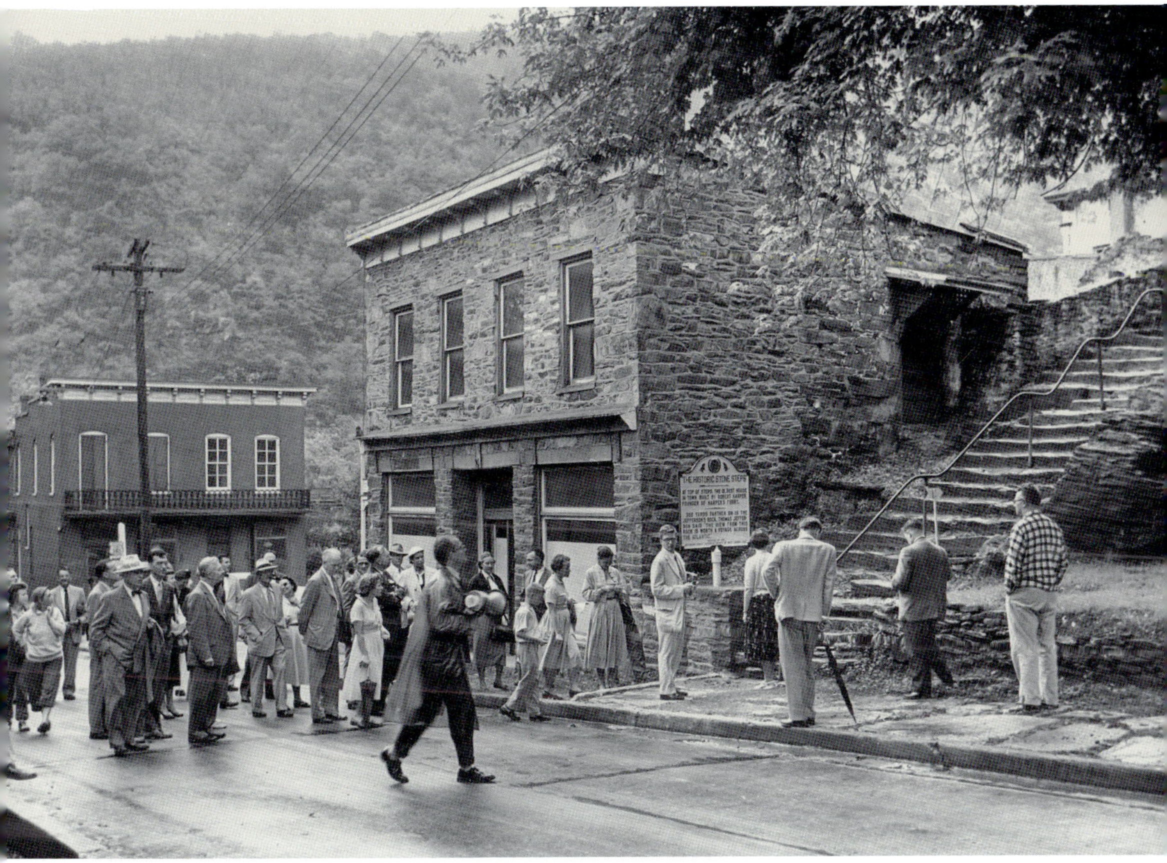

John Wager Jr. constructed the John T. Rieley Building between 1804 and 1813. In 1853, John T. Rieley's Boot and Shoe Manufactory was located here. All types of boots and shoes were produced, and all were guaranteed to be high quality. Today the building houses the Black Voices Museum, which depicts the struggles African Americans faced over the years.

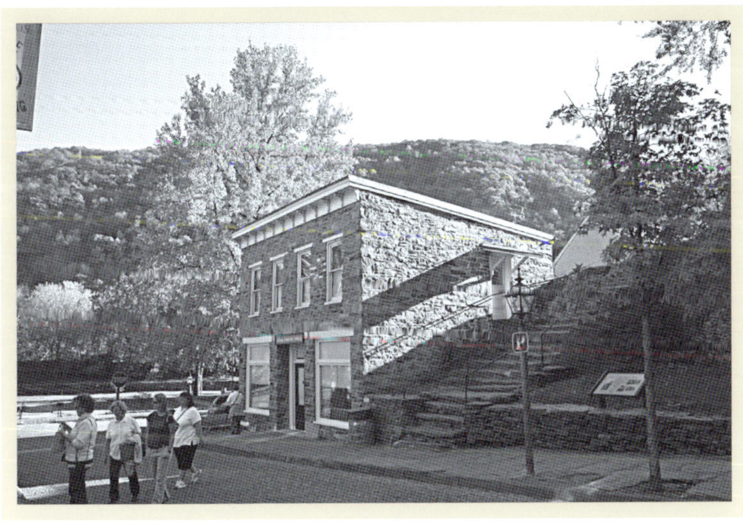

This tiny shop on the north side of High Street was Burton's Jewelry Store. The lot was purchased for $100 in 1857 by Alfred Burton, and he established a small jewelry store that sold and repaired watches, spectacles, and other jewelry. The building became dilapidated over the years, and the park service dismantled it. In 1991, it was restructured, and today the building is a replica of that first store.

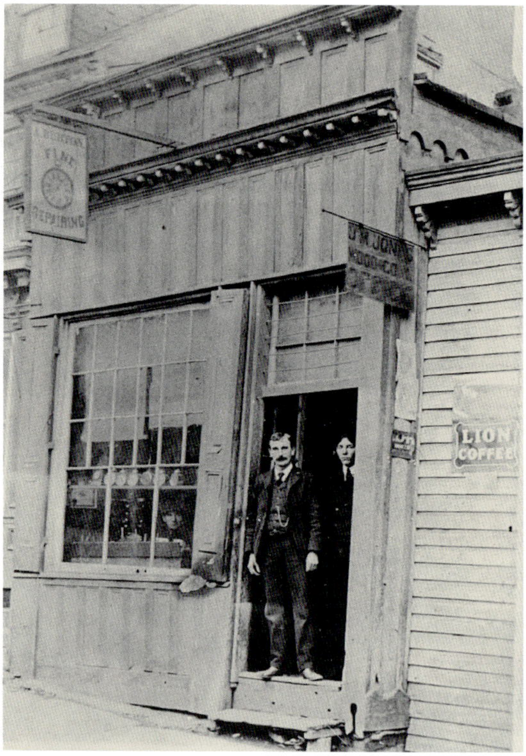

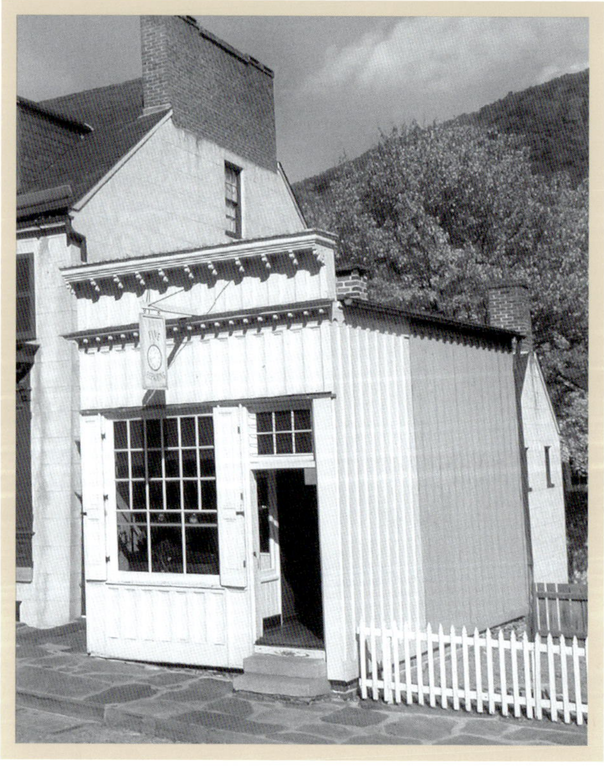

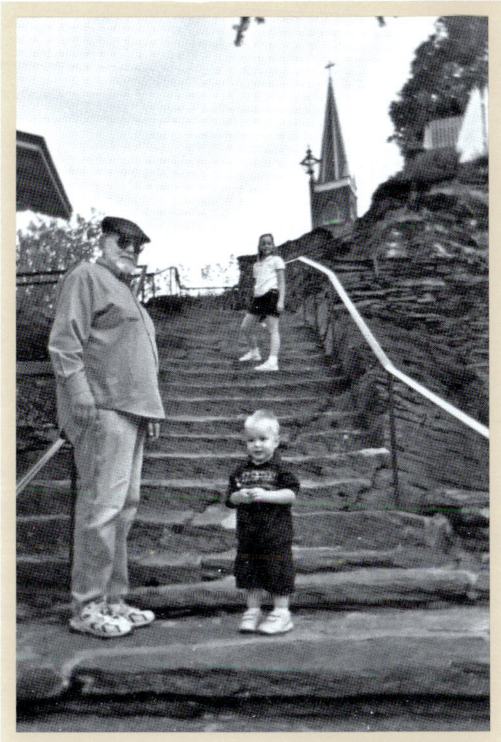

The Stone Steps are almost a trademark for Harpers Ferry. Everyone who comes to visit tries to ascend the steps to see Jefferson Rock. In the modern photograph, tourist Walter Wojcik appears with his grandson and granddaughter as they make the trek up to Jefferson Rock. In the *c.* 1865 photograph, no railings are present. They would come later as a safety measure.

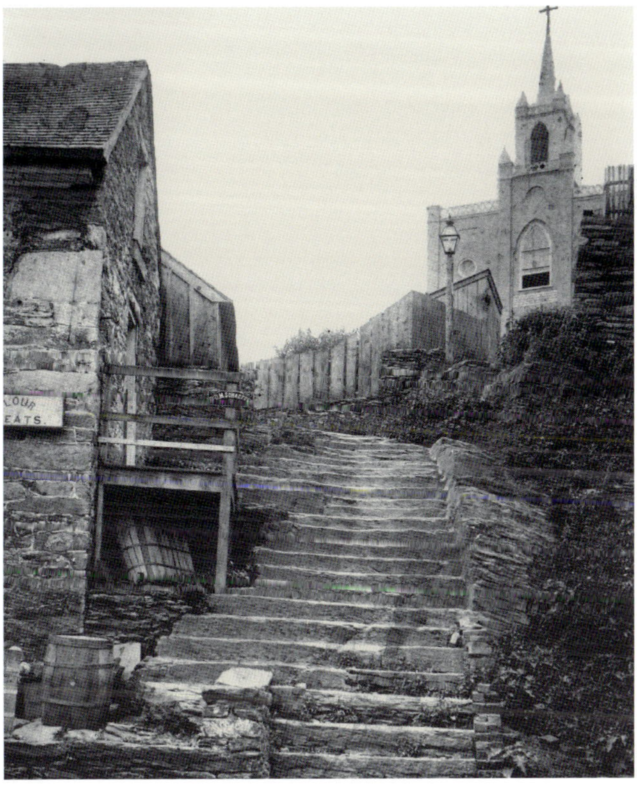

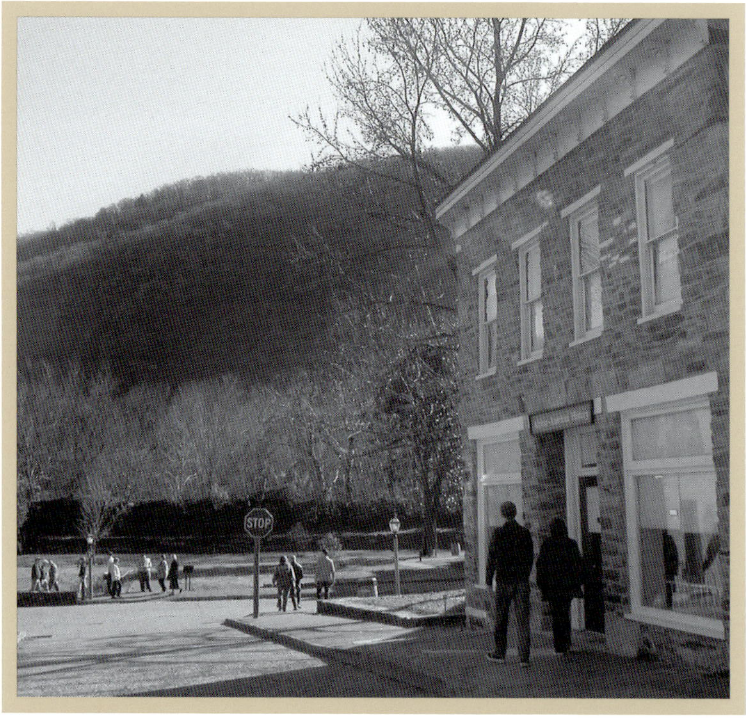

In the "then" photograph, people stand in the doorway of the John T. Rieley Building on the southwest side of High Street. The store sold "Fancy Groceries," as written on the window of the building. The building is one of the oldest in Harpers Ferry. Farther down and across the street, on the south side of Shenandoah Street, are two buildings that no longer exist as shown in the "now" photograph.

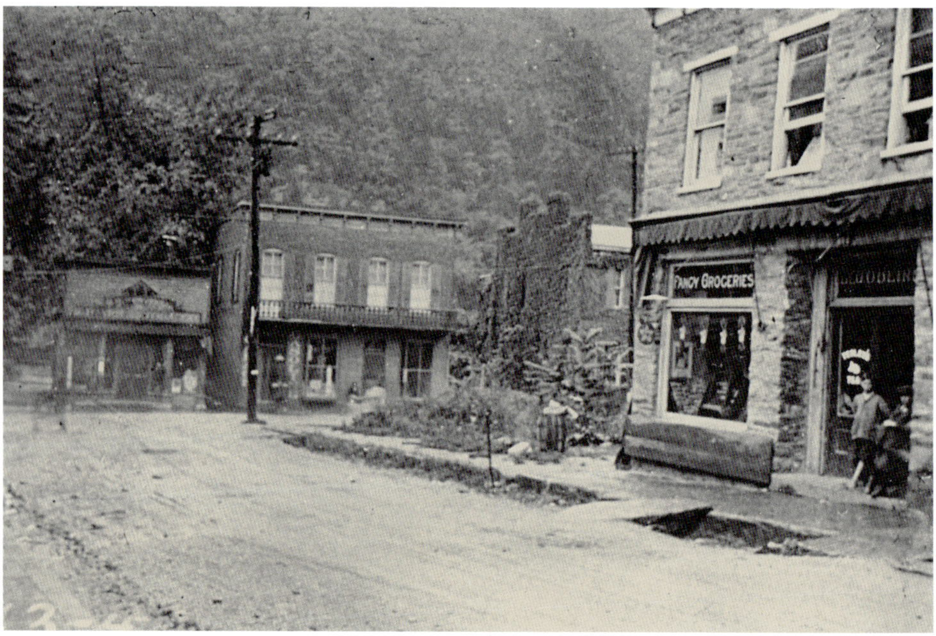

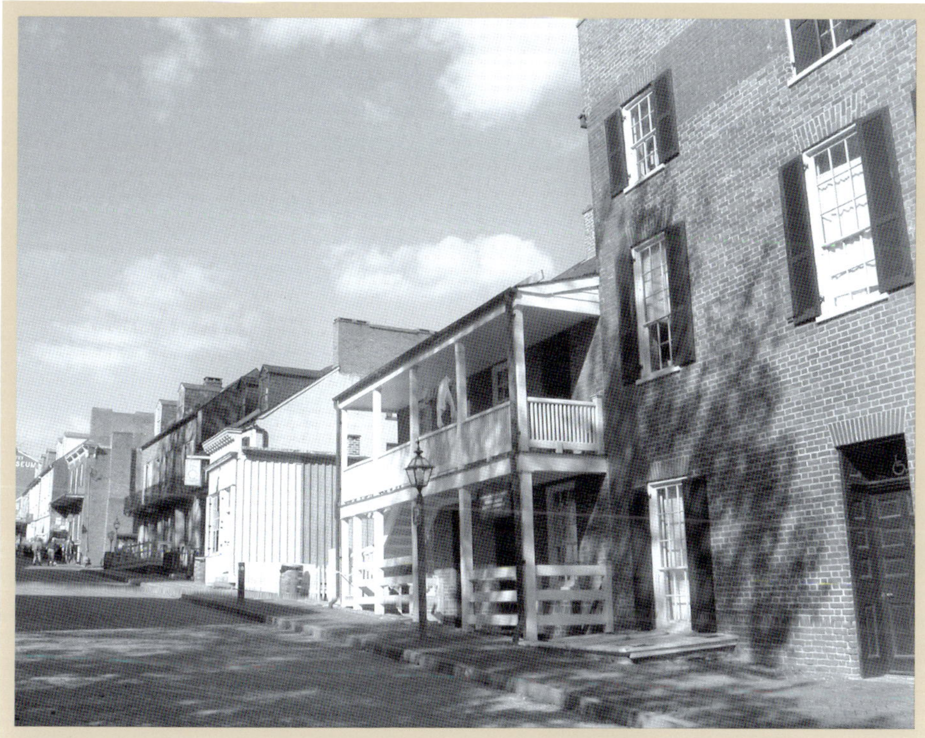

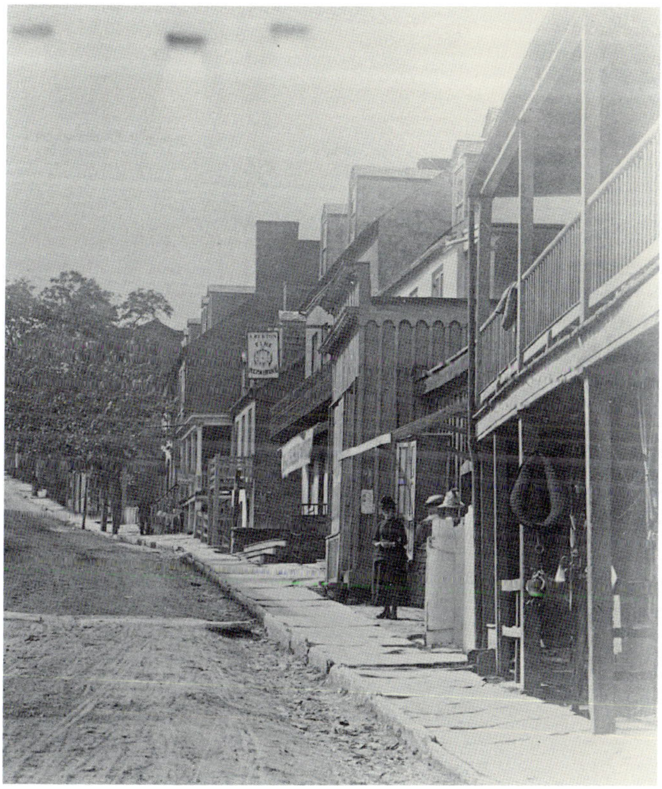

The north side of High Street is depicted in these photographs. The little white building is Burton's Jewelry Store. To the right of that is the Ann C. Stephenson Building. To the left, farther up the hill, is the Susan Downey House and beside that Frederick A. Roeder's Confectionery. The "then" photograph was taken in 1886 and depicts the still-unpaved street.

The "then" photograph of the southwestern side of High Street shows many more buildings than the "now" photograph does. The building visible in the "now" photograph is the Nichols-Williams Building, built by William B. Nichols between 1896 and 1907. Originally the building served as a grocery, but now it is home of the Civil War Museum. There were four buildings on this site prior to the erection of this structure.

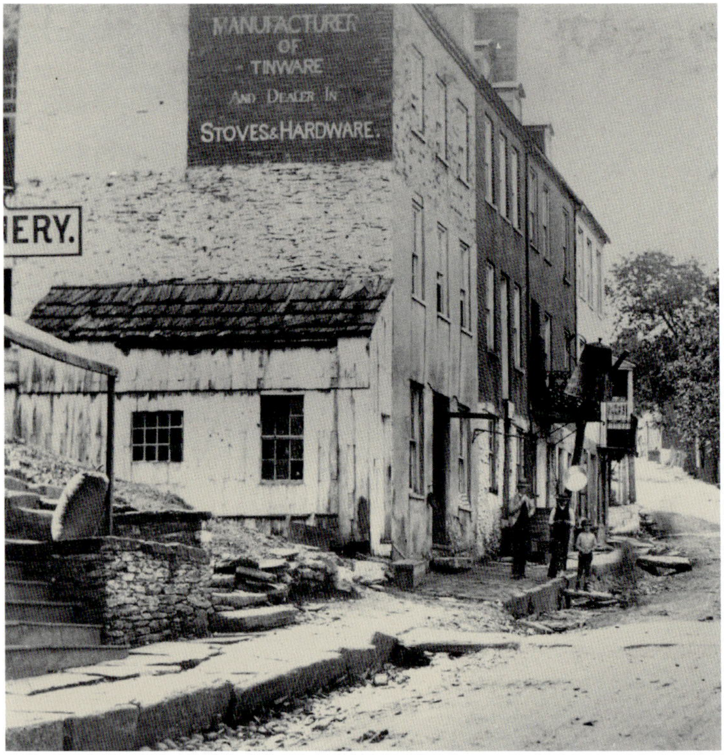

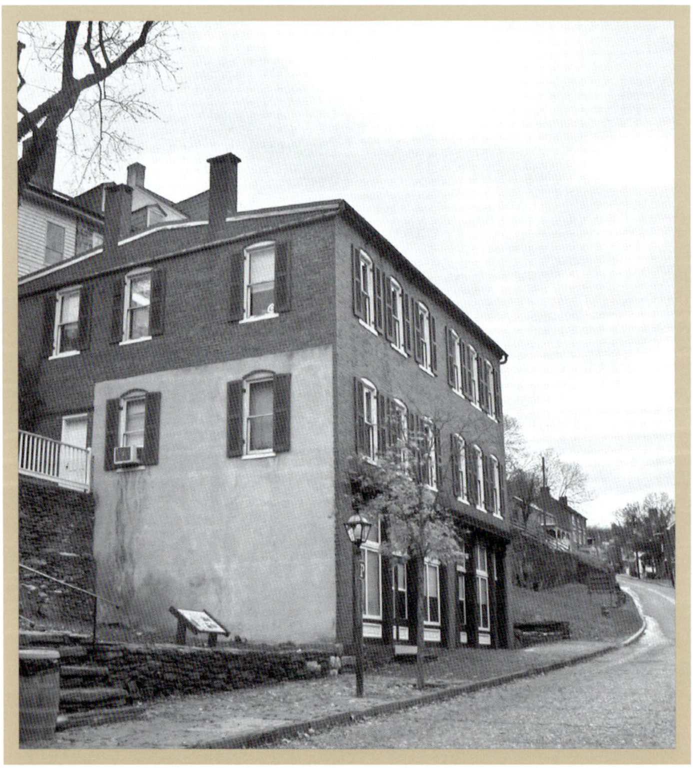

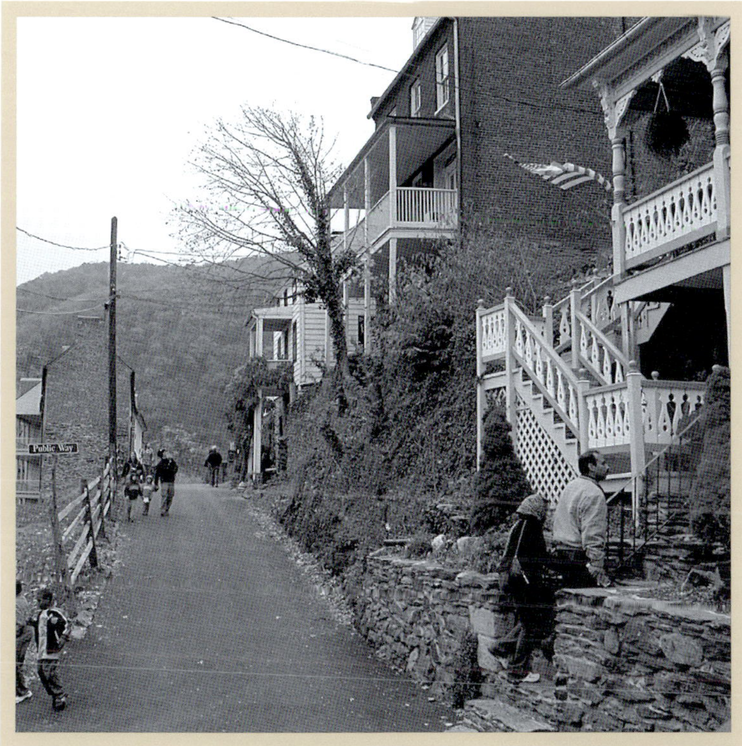

Paved streets have replaced dirt ones. Houses and buildings have been restored and refurbished to make Public Way an inviting lane. Today tourists can be seen regularly serenely strolling along this street. In the "then" photograph, a dog can be seen without a leash, something that is not allowed today with the leash law in effect in Harpers Ferry.

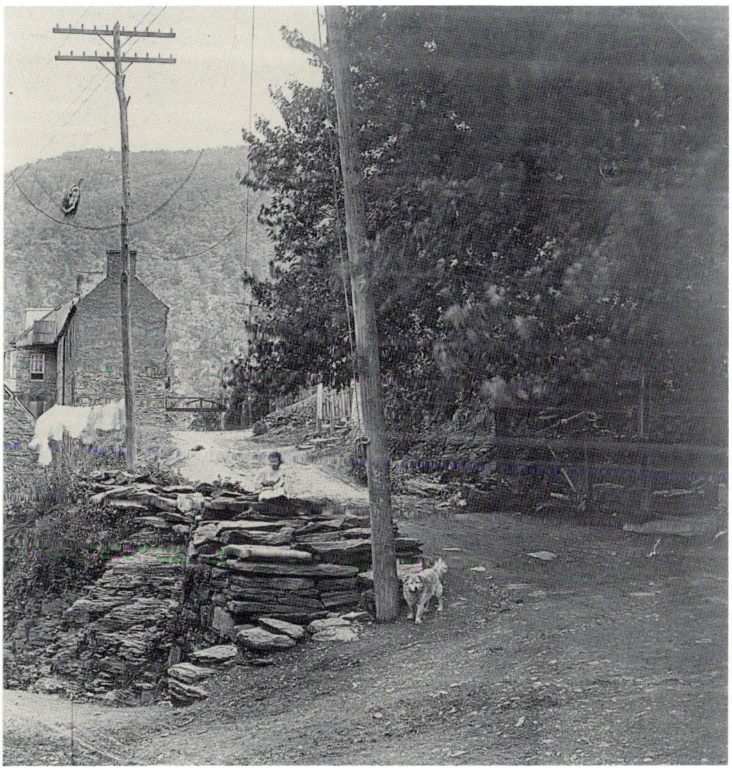

Looking down High Street in the "then" photograph, one can see buildings erected along the right side of the street. Today no such buildings exist, as the "now" photograph shows. The only buildings visible on the southeast side of the street are located further down the street and include the Nichols-Williams Building, while the southwest side of the street is filled with quaint and unusual shops for tourists.

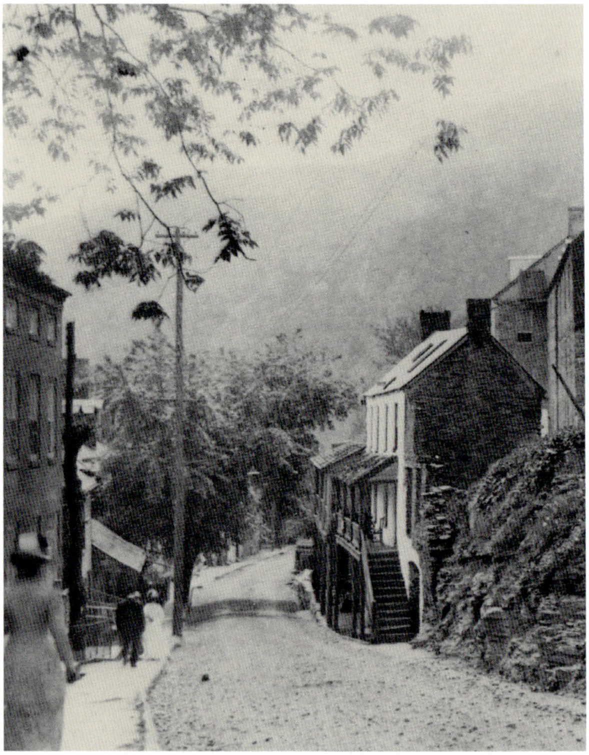

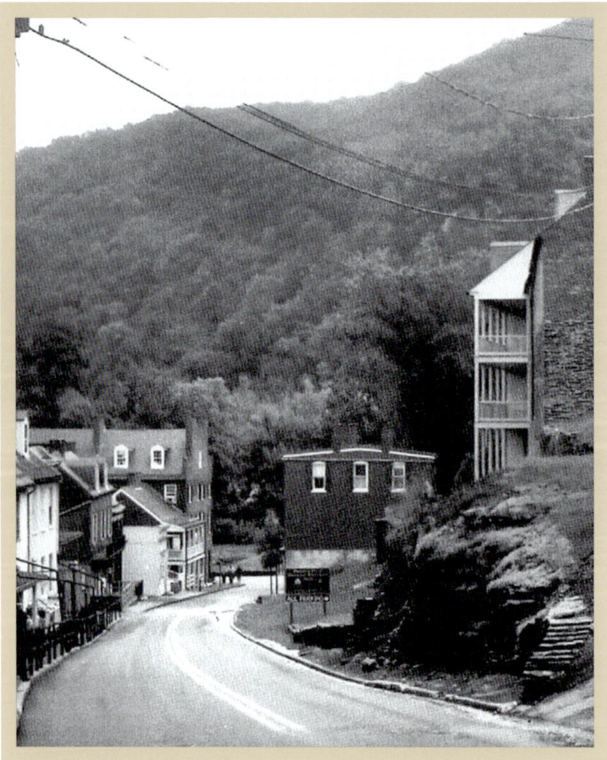

CHAPTER 3

MAXIMAL MILIEU

UPPER TOWN

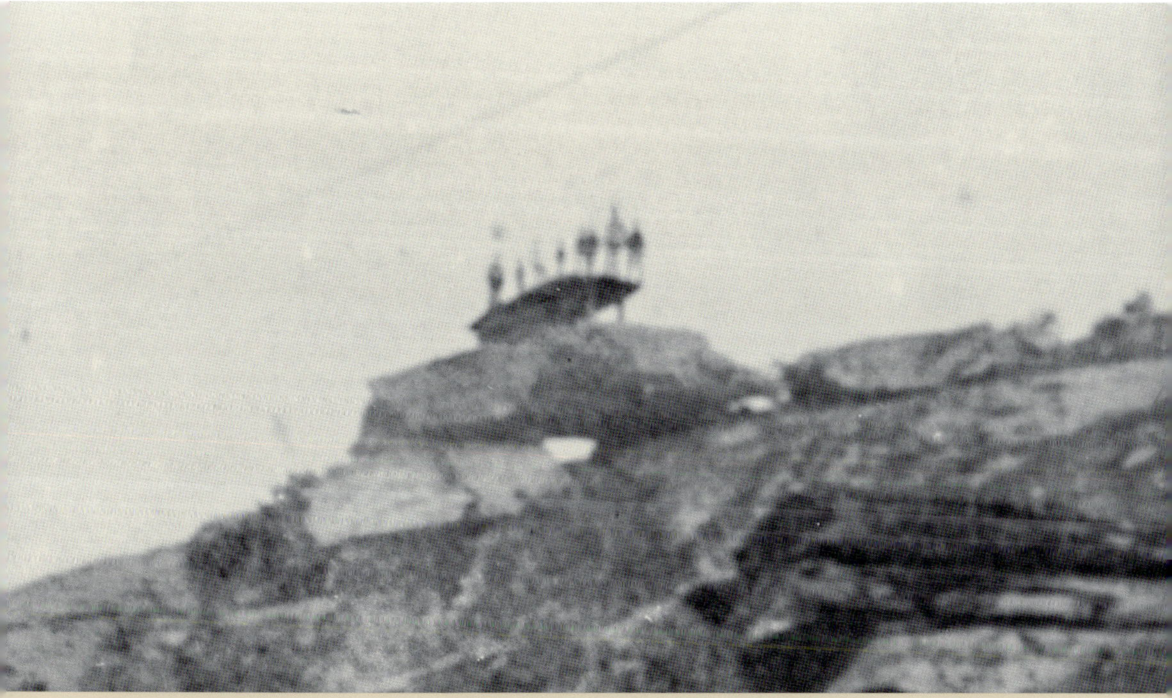

Pictured at the top of this 1865 photograph is Jefferson Rock, which is the apex of the Upper Town. The rock is the focus of many people's visits to Harpers Ferry. Many remember the statement by Thomas Jefferson that the view from atop Jefferson Rock is worth the voyage across the Atlantic. In this photograph, people can be seen standing on the rock, which is not allowed today.

While Hog Alley is actually part of Lower Town, it connects to High Street, which leads to Upper Town and is included here for that reason. In the "then" photograph, all visible buildings appear to be very dilapidated and in desperate need of repair and restoration. In the "now" photograph, that restoration has been completed. On the left is the building that housed Frederick A. Roeder's Confectionery. In the middle in the background are the Marmion Tenant Houses.

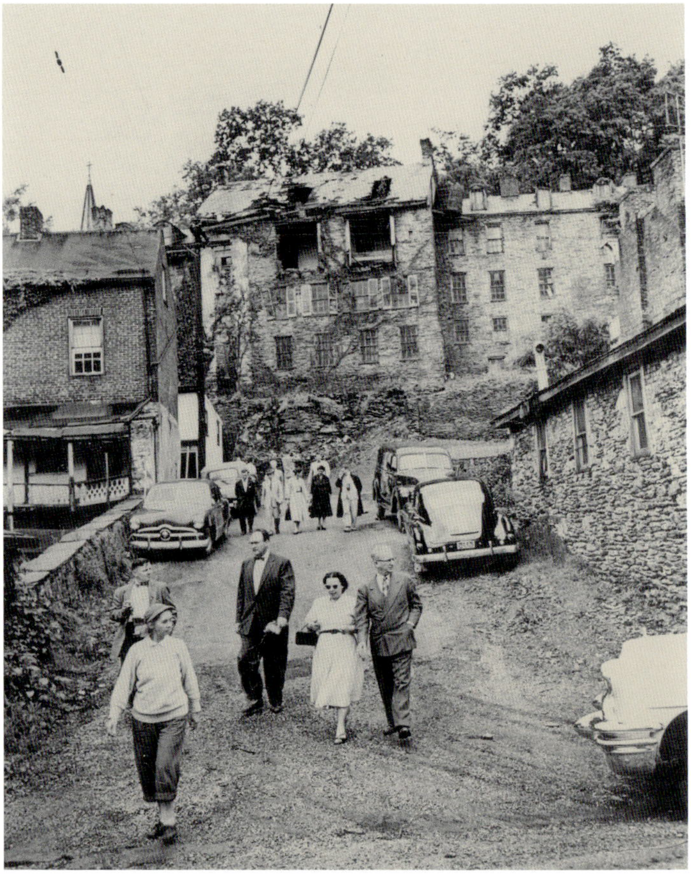

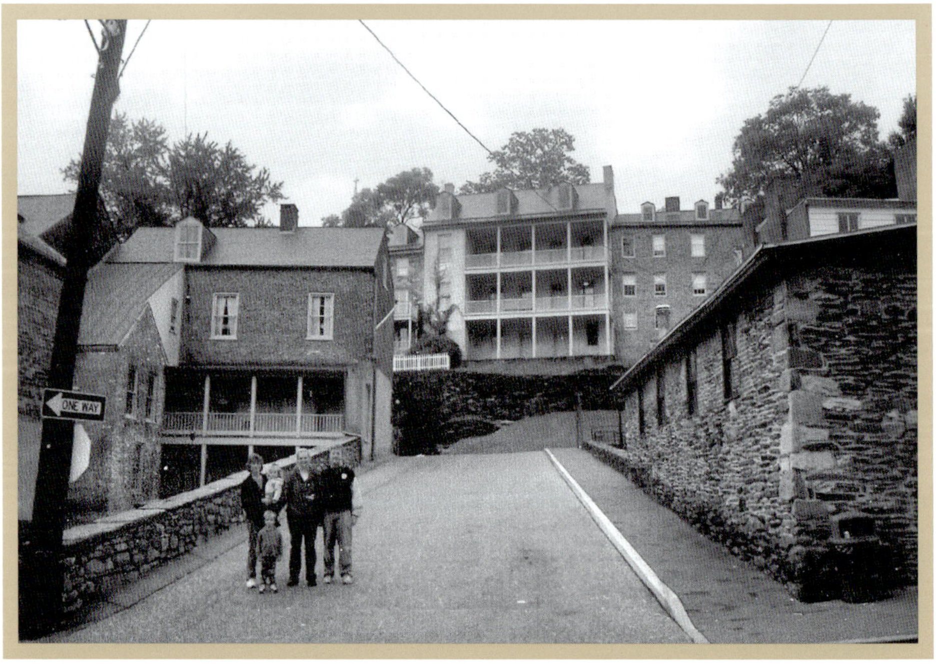

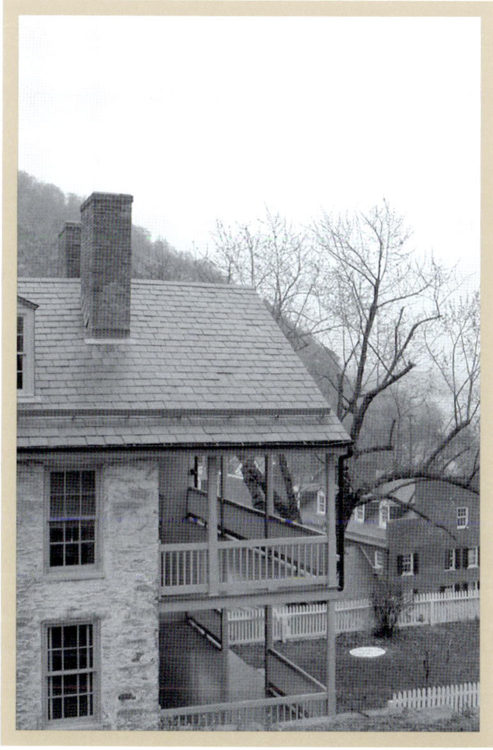

Originally serving as the town's first tavern, Harper House was begun by Robert Harper in 1775. It was built of stone on the side of the hill and was not completed until 1782 because of a labor shortage. Harper died that October and never occupied the house. Pictured on the bridge to the Harper Garden are neighbors of the Marmions. Taken around 1910, the bridge appears to be sturdy. In the "now" photograph, there is no bridge visible.

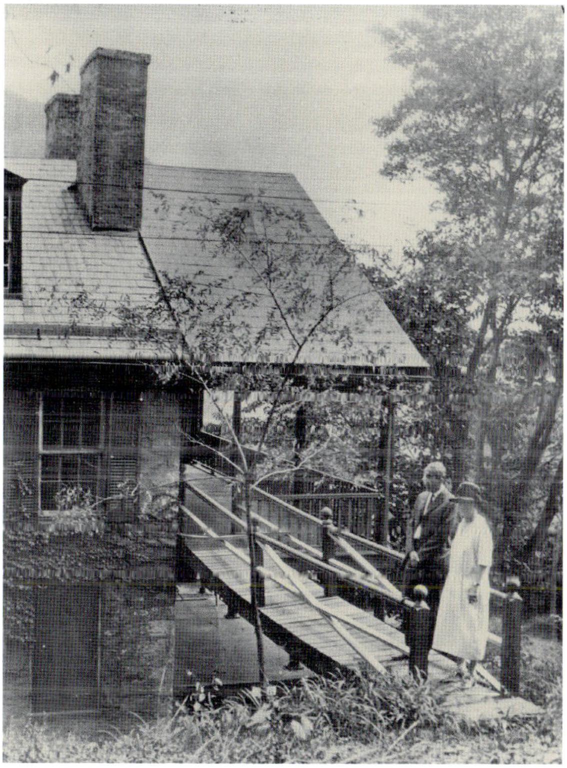

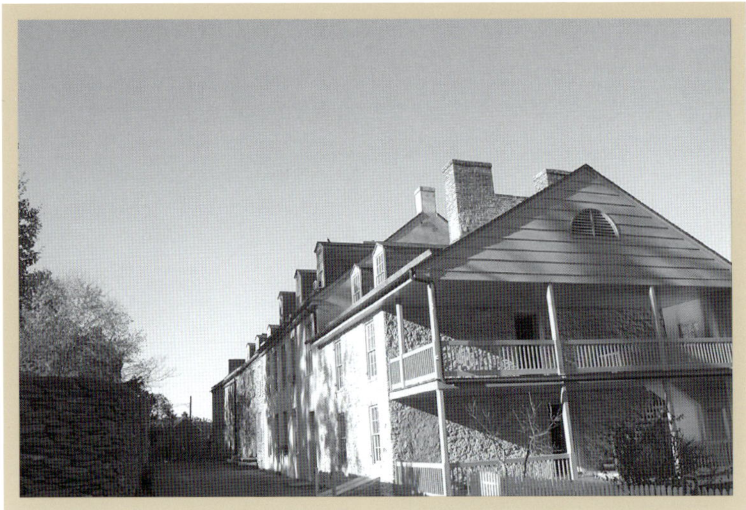

The man who began the construction of the Harper House, Robert Harper, died before he was ever able to dwell in it. After having come to the area in 1747 to construct a meetinghouse for the Quakers, he purchased "The Hole" from Peter Stephens, and it became Harpers Ferry. Over the years, the house fell into disrepair. Eventually it was restored by the National Park Service. Harper was buried in Harper Cemetery in the Upper Town.

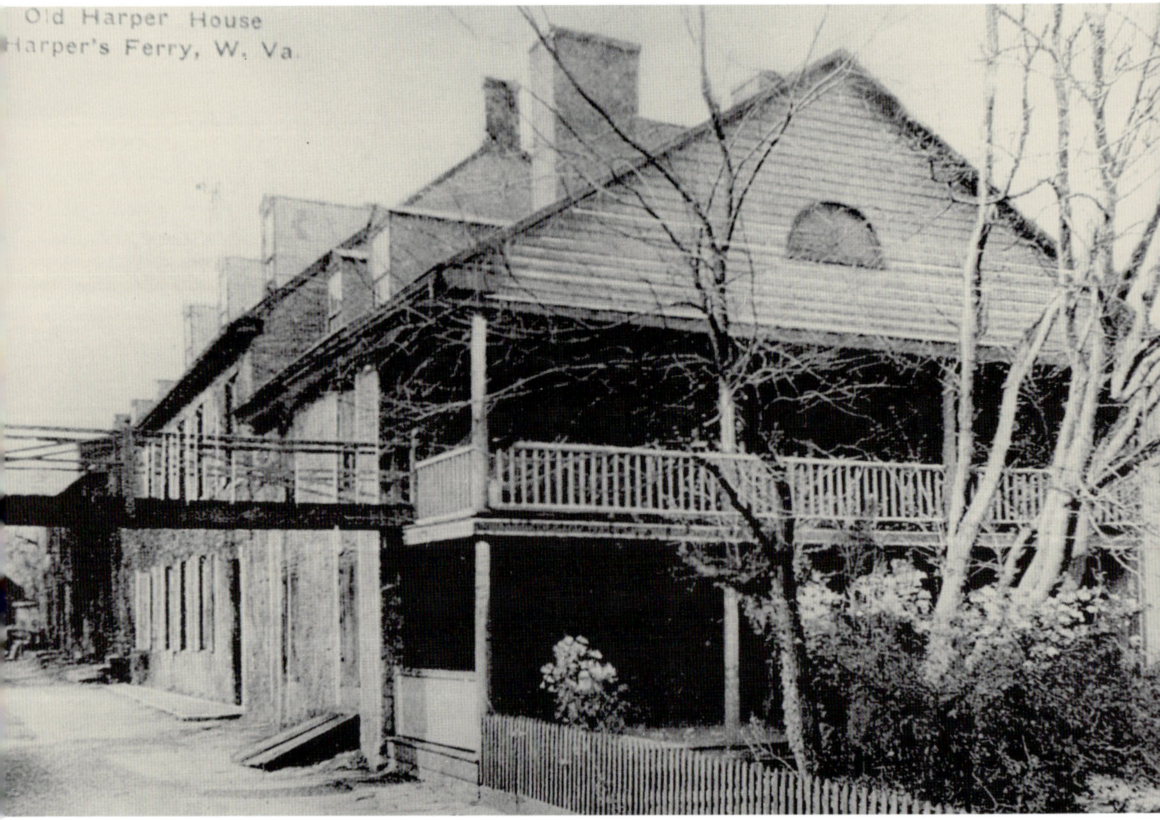

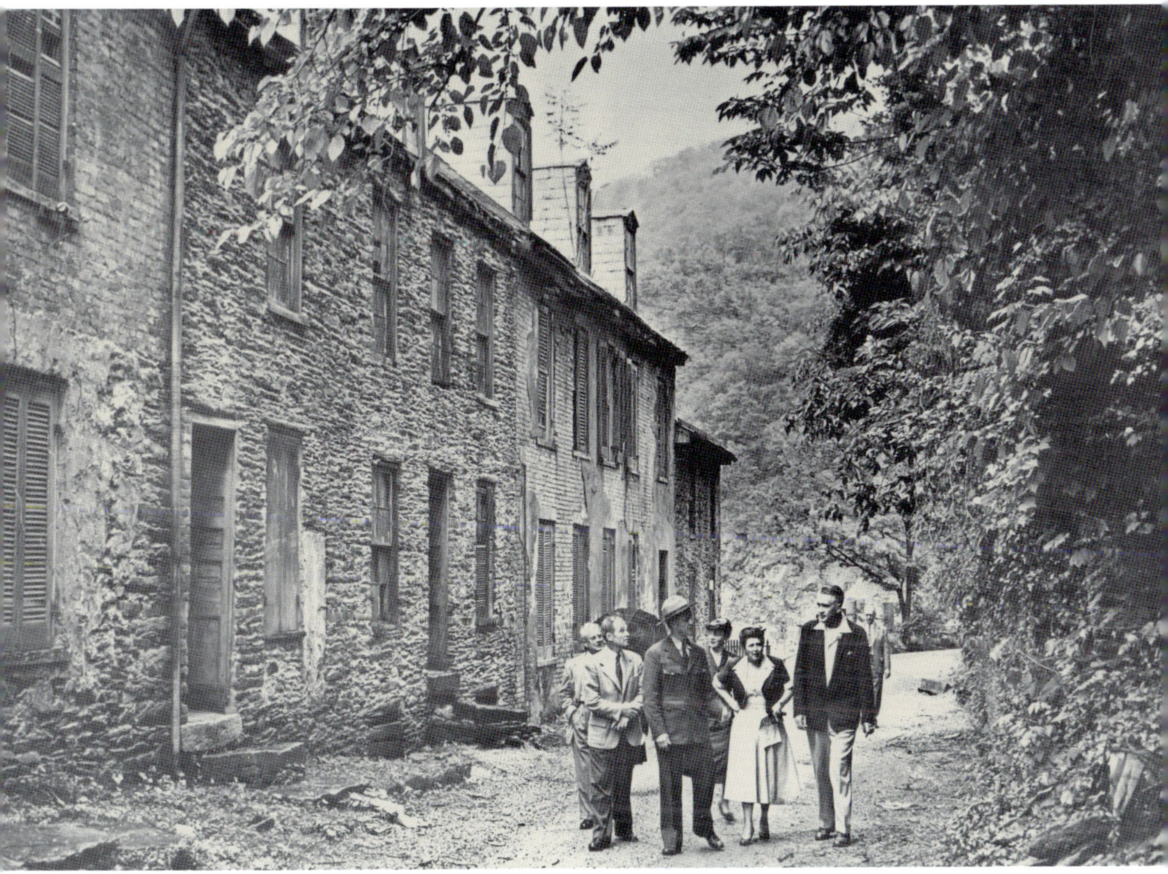

The restored Marmion Tenement Houses are today used by the National Park Service. Constructed of sturdy materials, the buildings were restored and refurbished by the National Park Service. In the "then" photograph, much vegetation has taken over. The road was dirt and stone, as it remains today. Farther down Public Way, where it meets High Street, it is paved.

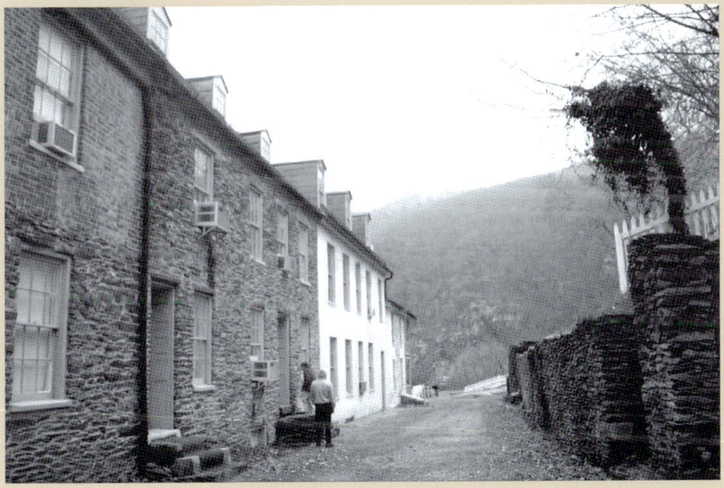

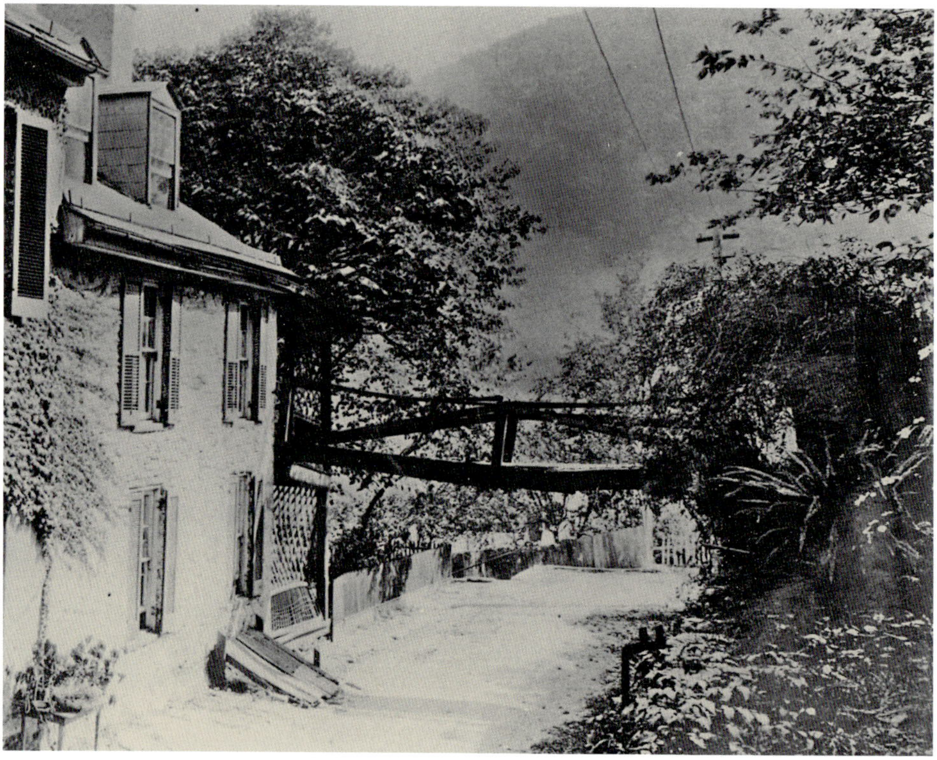

The wall for the Harper Garden to the right has lasted many years. The facade of the Harper House shown in the "now" photograph was refurbished by the National Park Service after the town was made a national historical park. The bridge in the "then" photograph is long since gone. Today visitors may walk up the road to the right, at the end of the wall, to visit St. Peter's Catholic Church on the way to Jefferson Rock.

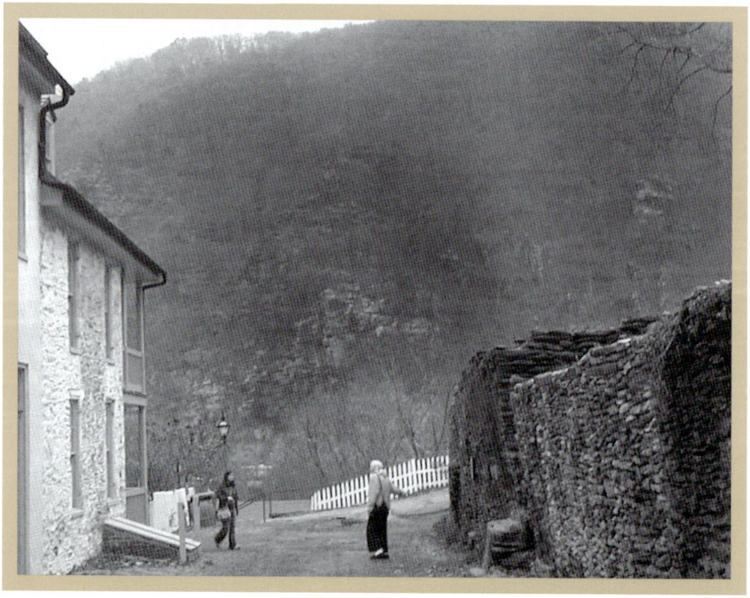

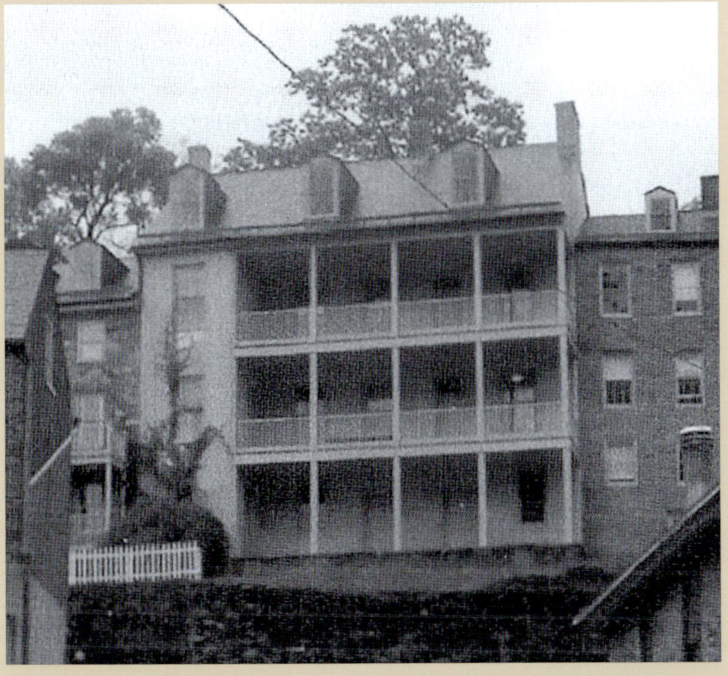

Pictured in a state of monumental disrepair in the "then" photograph is Marmion Hall, located between the Harper House and the second Marmion Tenant House along Public Way. The "now" photograph shows the appearance after restoration and refurbishment by the National Park Service. Today the National Park Service uses the building for offices for both volunteers and employees.

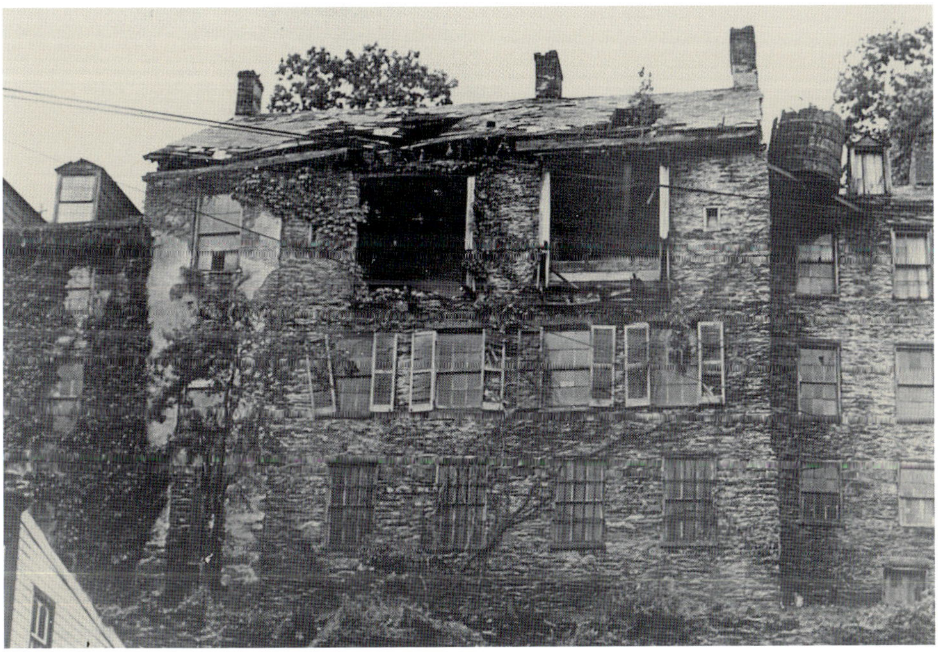

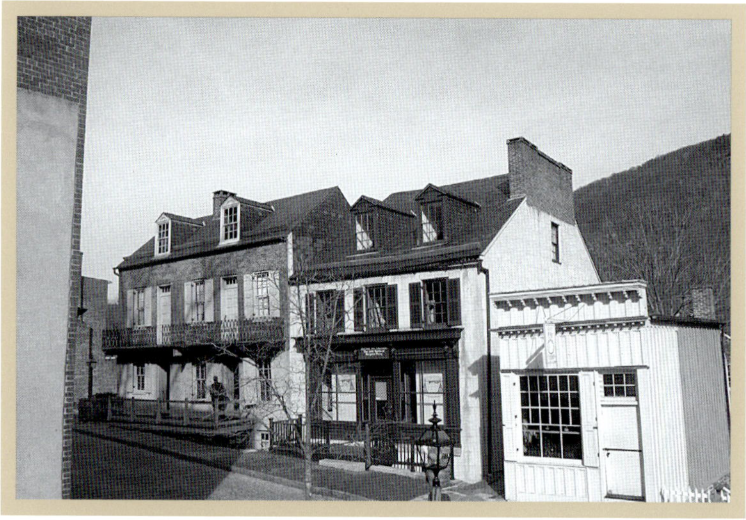

Built between 1838 and 1839, the Susan Downey House was so named because she purchased the lot on which it sits. The lot was part of the original Wager Reservation. The builder was William Anderson, and the house has served many purposes in its lifetime. Today it houses shops and store that both tourists and locals frequent.

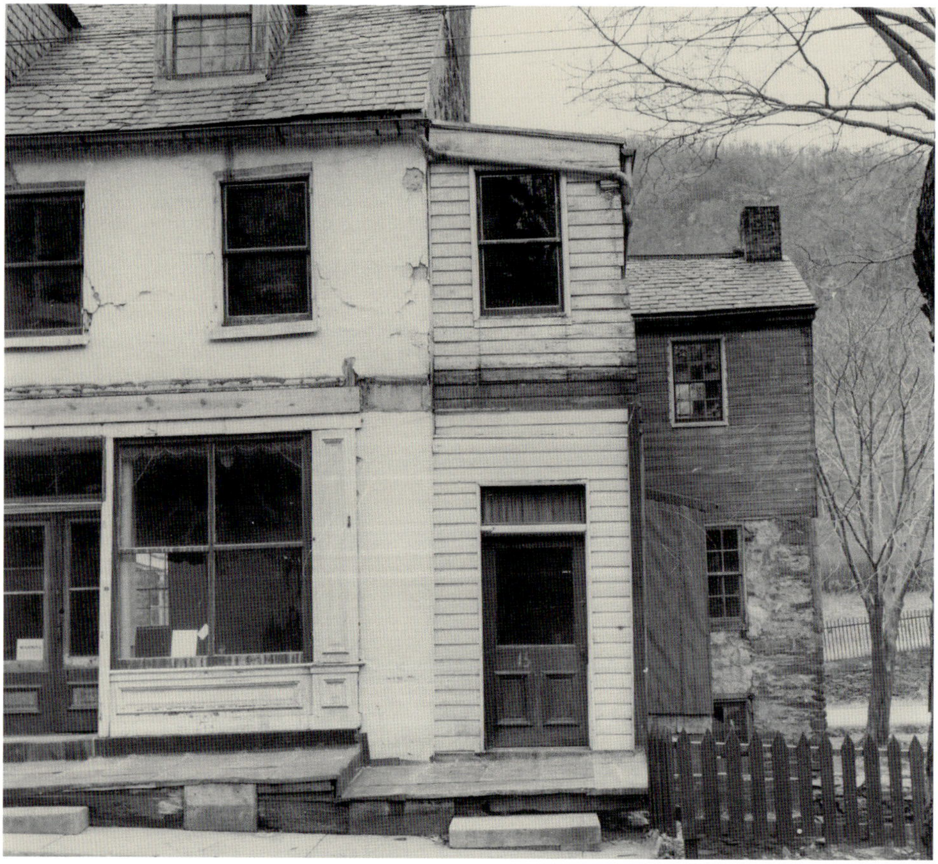

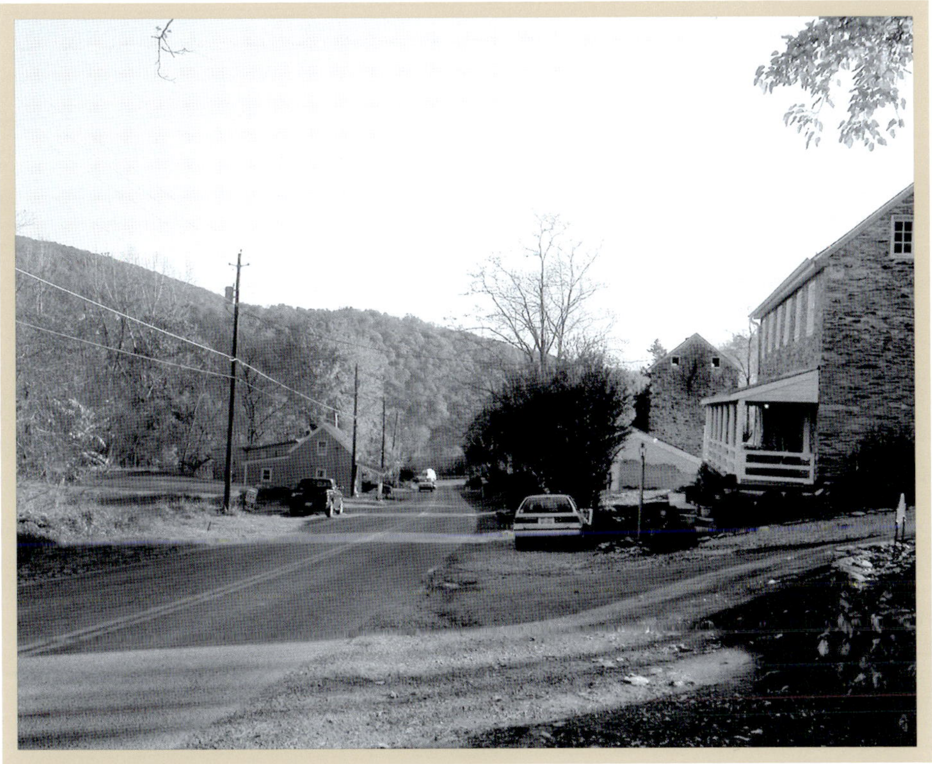

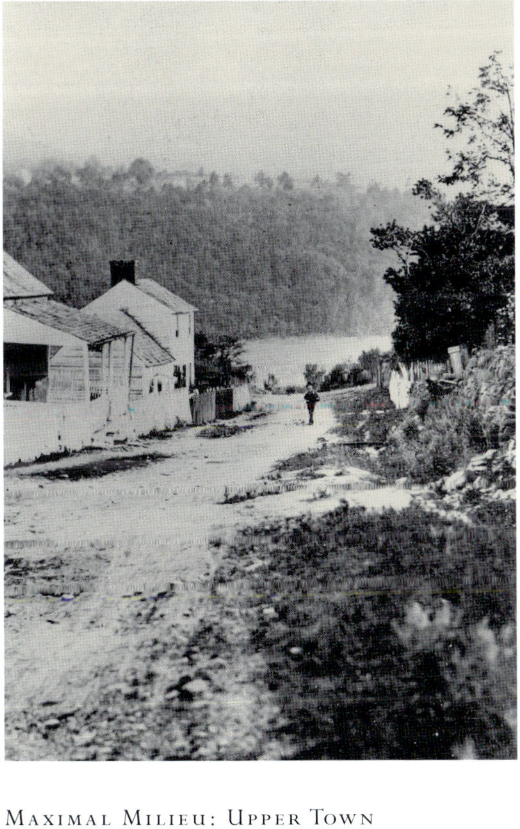

The lower end of Union Street can be seen in this 1886 photograph. Taken on May 29, 1886, the photograph shows the Shenandoah River in the distance along with Loudoun Heights. The dirt road has houses on both sides and a man walking. The modern photograph shows a paved road, and the river is no longer visible because of overgrown vegetation. However, Loudoun Heights is clearly seen in the distance. In addition, at the bottom of the hill, Union Street stops when it reaches Route 340. In neither photograph is the steep grade of the road as evident as it is in reality.

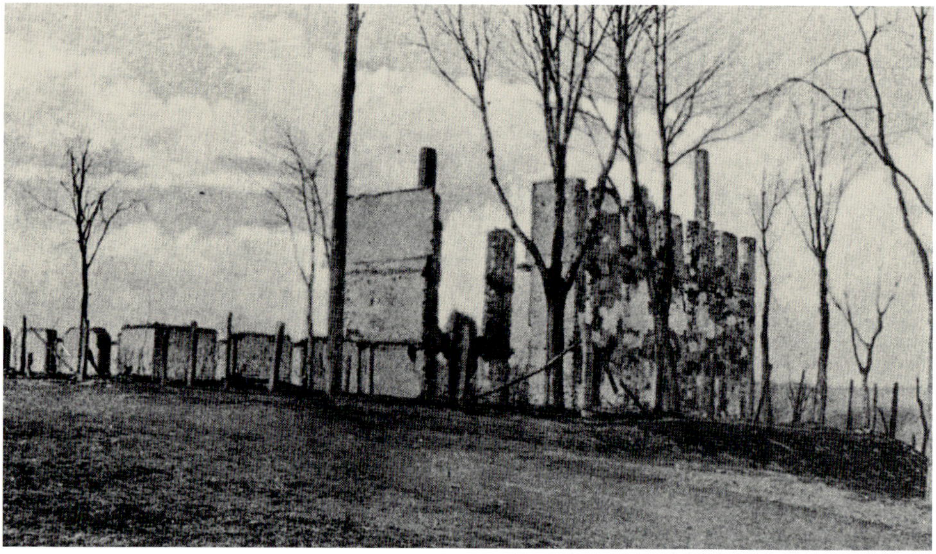

On December 11, 1912, the Hilltop House Hotel was destroyed by fire. It was later rebuilt, as shown in the "now" photograph. The hotel has had interesting guests such as Alexander Graham Bell, Mark Twain, Pearl S. Buck, and Pres. Woodrow Wilson. John Brown's raid would take place 30 years before the Hilltop House was founded. Today it welcomes guests to enjoy its quaint charm and gorgeous views.

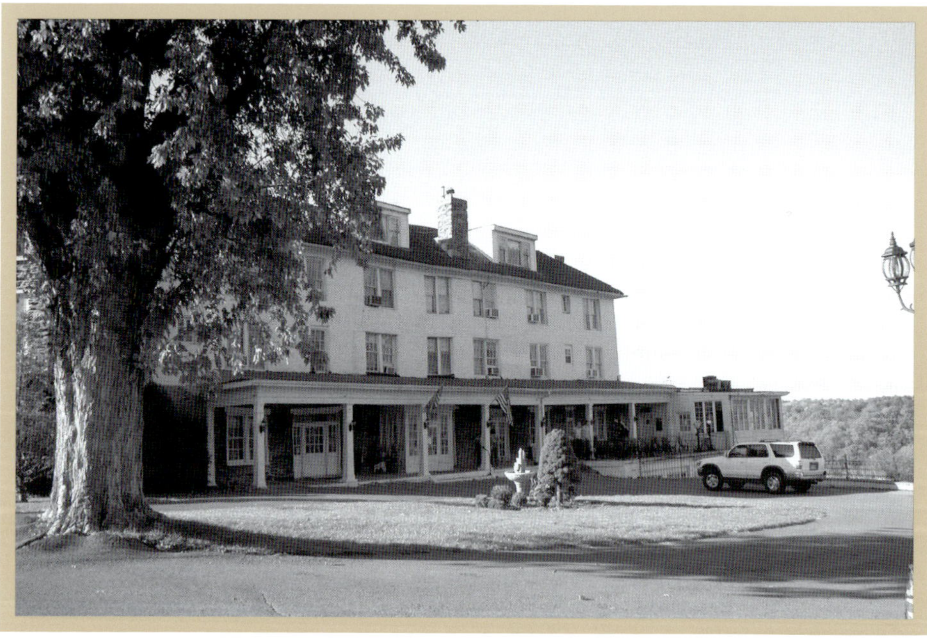

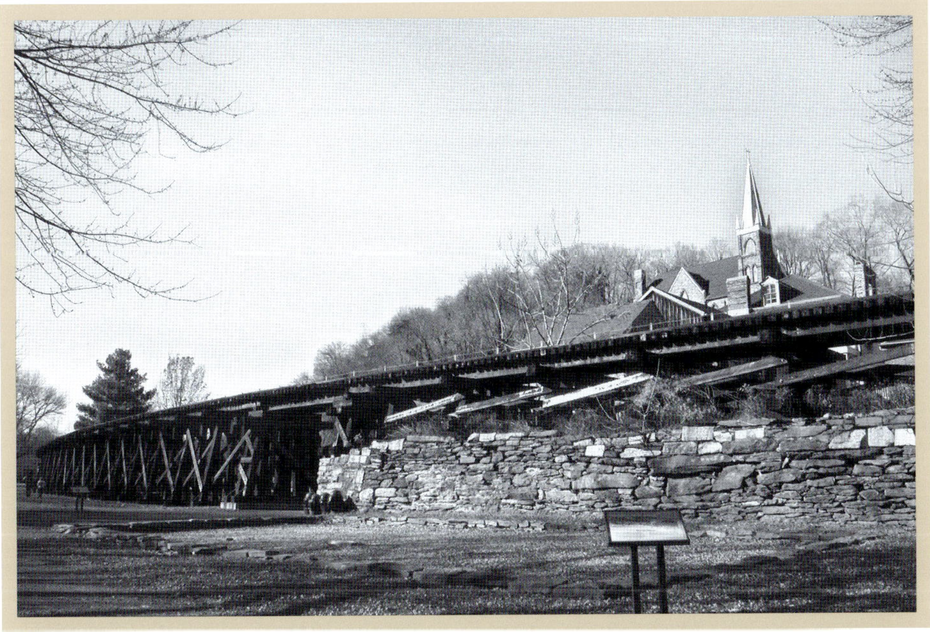

Between 1846 and 1847, the Market House was built on government property. It was 30 feet wide and 60 feet long, and the flood of 1936 destroyed it. Twice a week on Saturday and Wednesday, a town market was held on the first floor, where Upper and Lower Town goods such as meats, cheeses, fruits, vegetables, eggs, fish, and poultry were sold by locals for 21 years starting in 1847. The "now" photograph shows only the foundation outline.

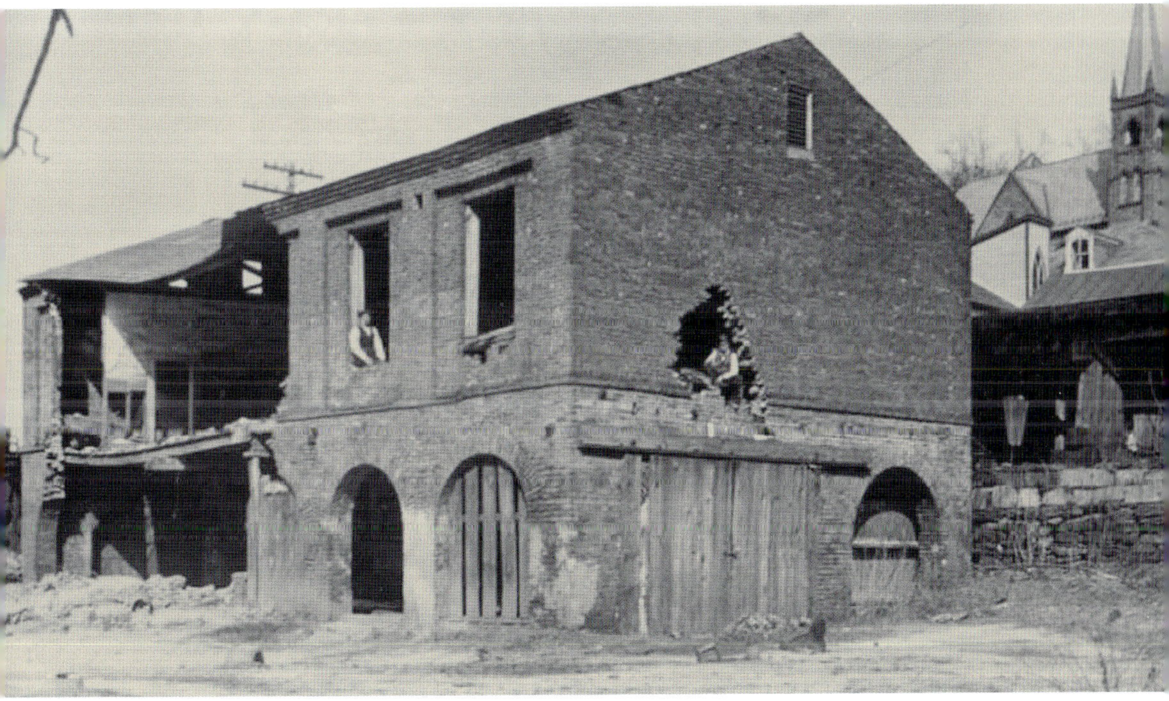

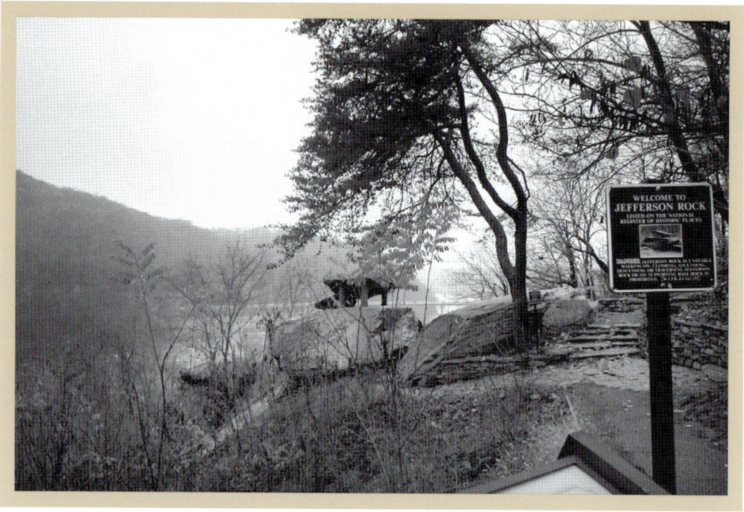

These two pages show photographs of Jefferson Rock, looking both upriver and downriver. The "then" photograph looking up the Shenandoah was taken on May 29, 1886. People can be seen standing on top of Jefferson Rock. It was Thomas Jefferson who made this rock famous when he stated that a view from atop the rock looking down the river was worth the voyage across the Atlantic. The "now" photograph, taken over 100 years later, shows the rock and a view obscured by vegetation.

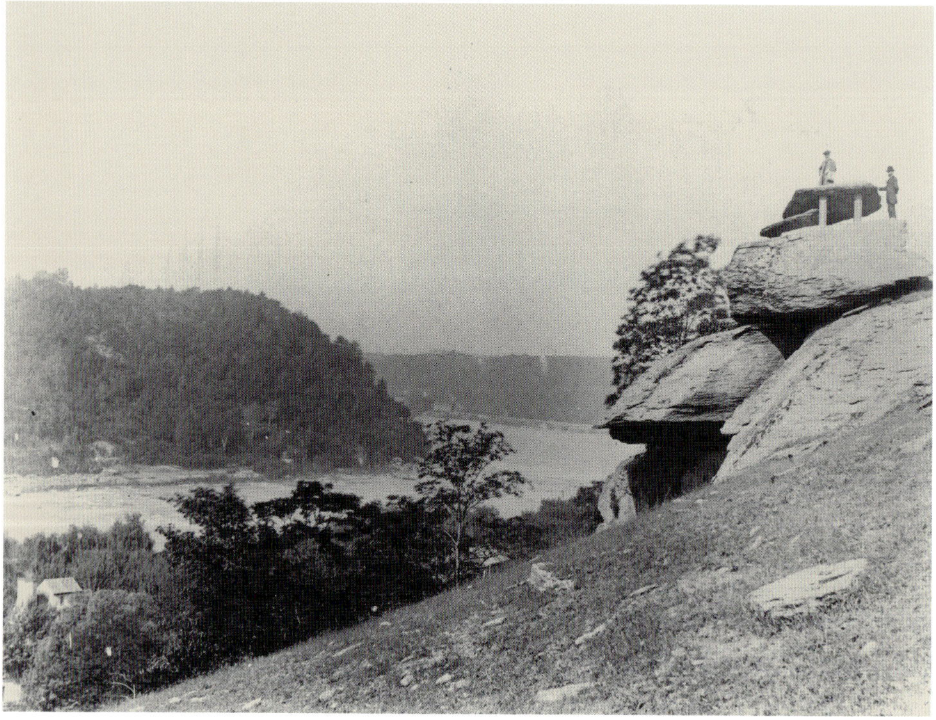

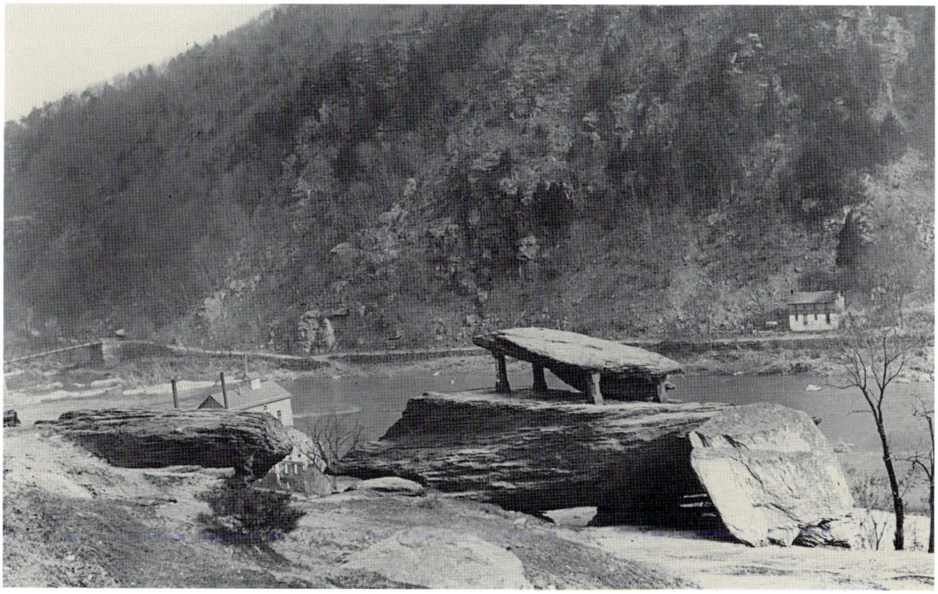

Taken from Camp Hill, the "then" photograph was taken March 10, 1876. It shows Jefferson Rock, the Shenandoah River looking downstream, and the base of Loudoun Heights. The "now" photograph shows the same except in the middle of the photograph on the opposite side is Route 340. The bridge across the Potomac River can also be seen on the extreme left side of the photograph. In both photographs, the rock is supported. Originally there were no supports under the rock, and it moved when people stood atop it.

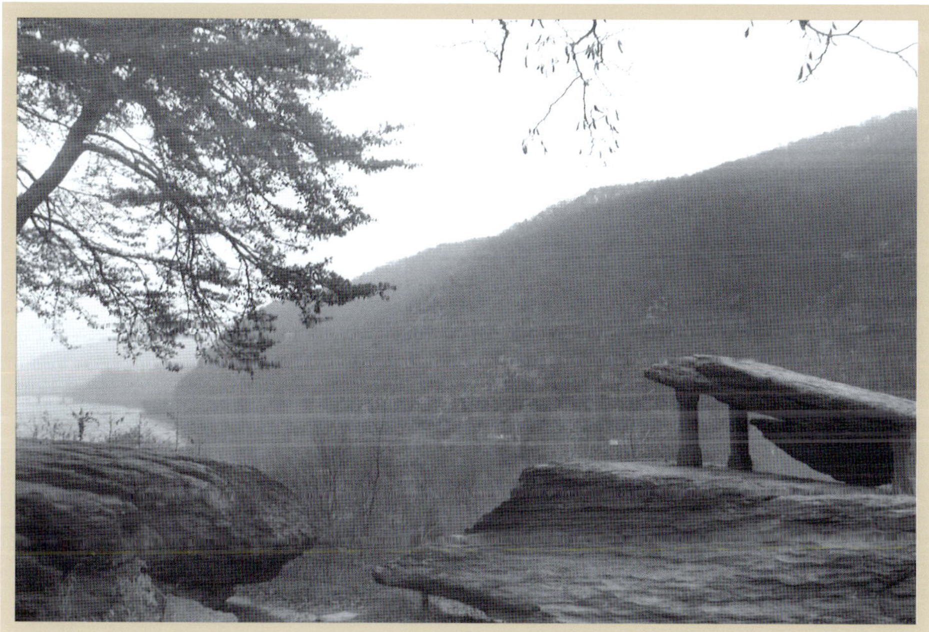

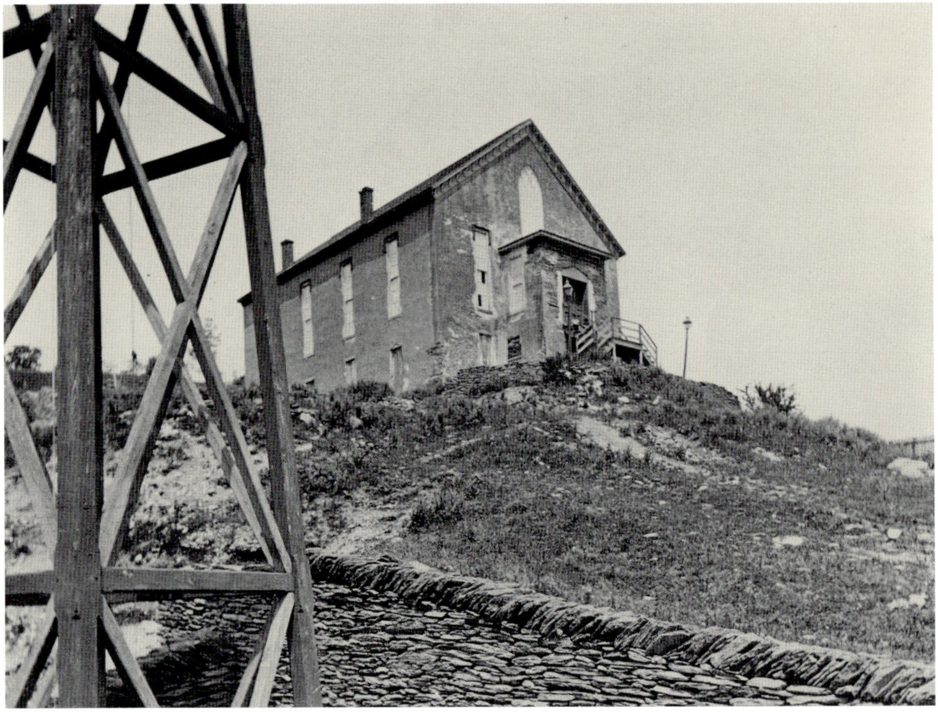

Taken May 29, 1886, the "then" photograph shows St. John's Protestant Episcopal Church. In 1825, the town's first church, the Free Church, was built on this lot, but it burned 20 years later. St. John's was built between 1851 and 1852 and was used as a hospital during parts of the Civil War. Severely damaged during the Civil War, in 1895, the church was sold and later abandoned. The "now" photograph shows only the skeletal remains.

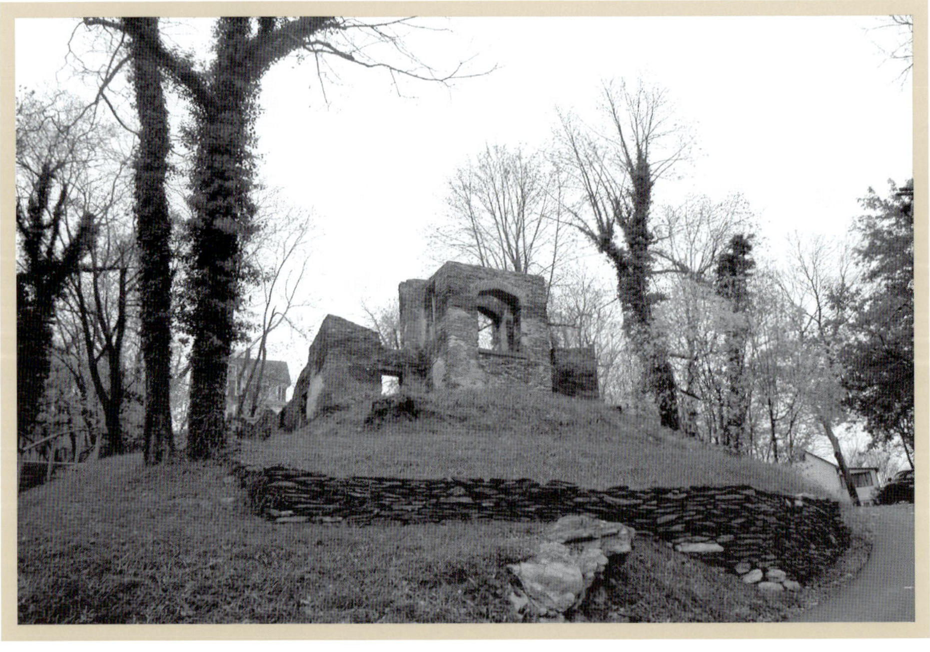

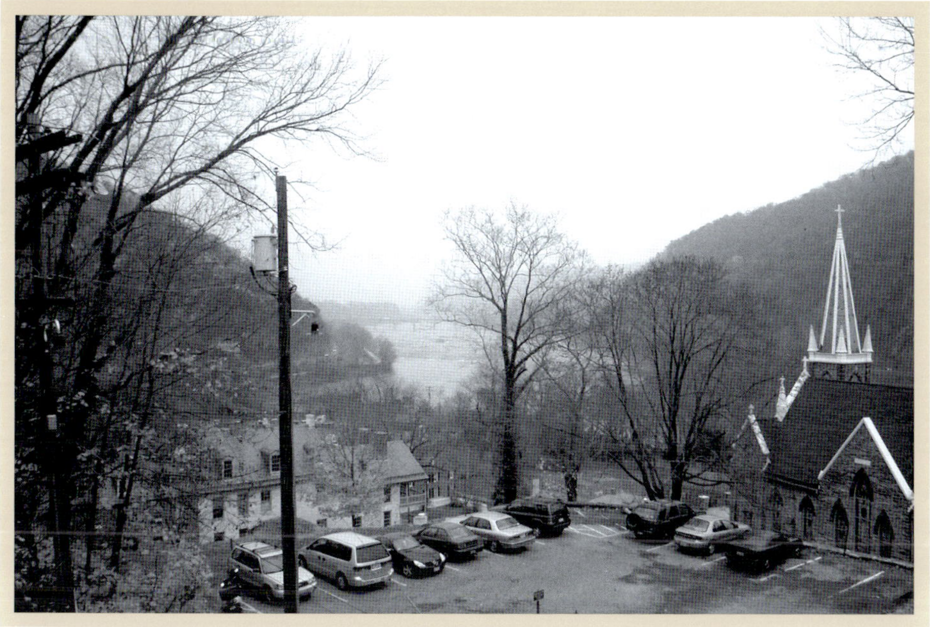

The "then" photograph of the Gap was taken from behind St. John's and shows very little vegetation obscuring the view. The "now" photograph was taken from the front steps of the church in order to get a view that was not obscured by dense vegetation. The church to the right is St. Peter's Roman Catholic Church, which was the only church that held religious services throughout the Civil War.

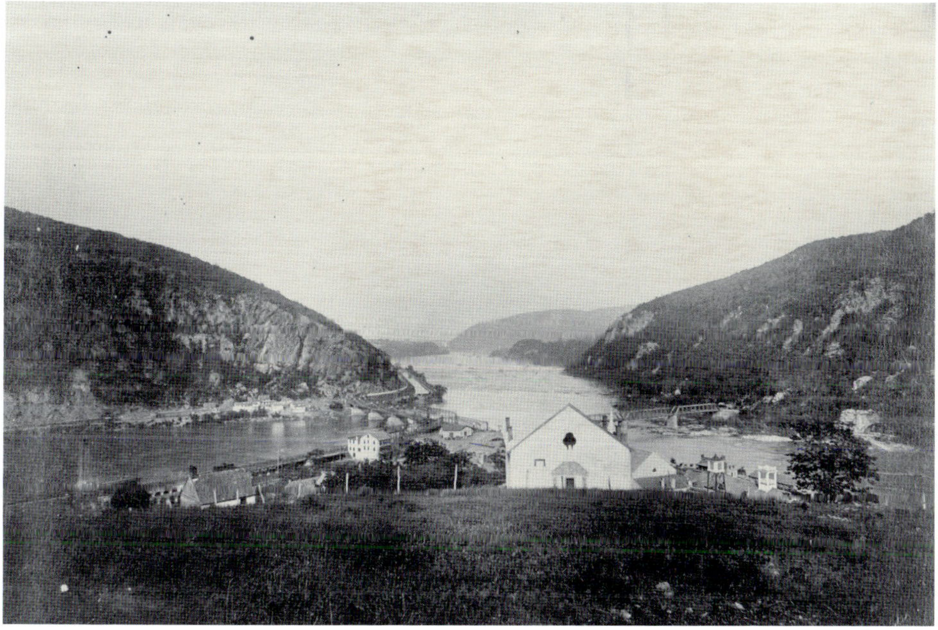

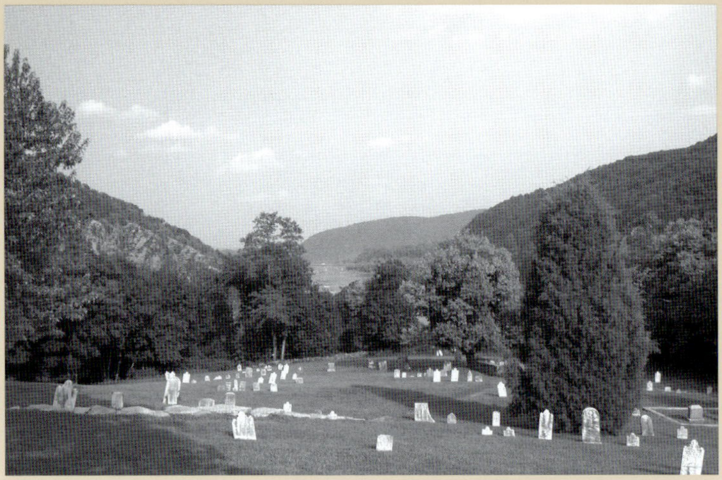

Following Robert Harper's death in 1782, a four-acre tract was set aside as a cemetery. Harper and several members of the Wager family are buried here. The "then" photograph shows a clear, unobstructed view of the Potomac River after the Shenandoah River has joined it. The "now" photograph shows the same view but with trees partially obscuring that view. Many of the tombstones and grave markers are deteriorating. In another 50 years, how much more vegetation will obstruct the view?

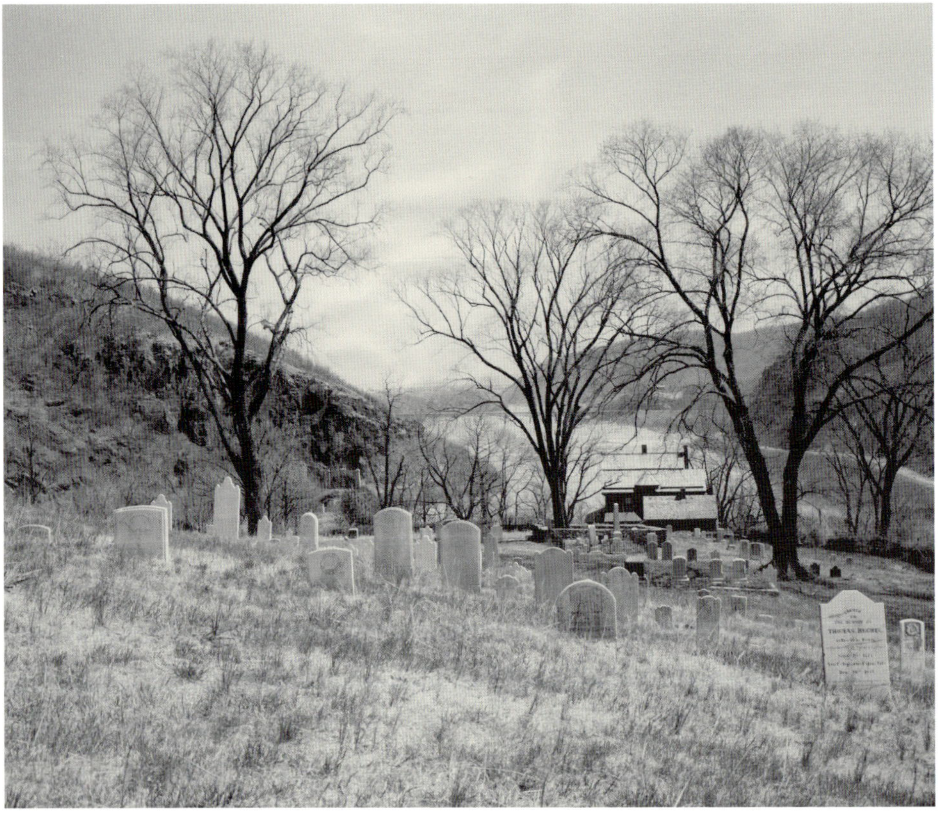

CHAPTER 4

JUSTIFIABLE PEDAGOGY

STORER COLLEGE

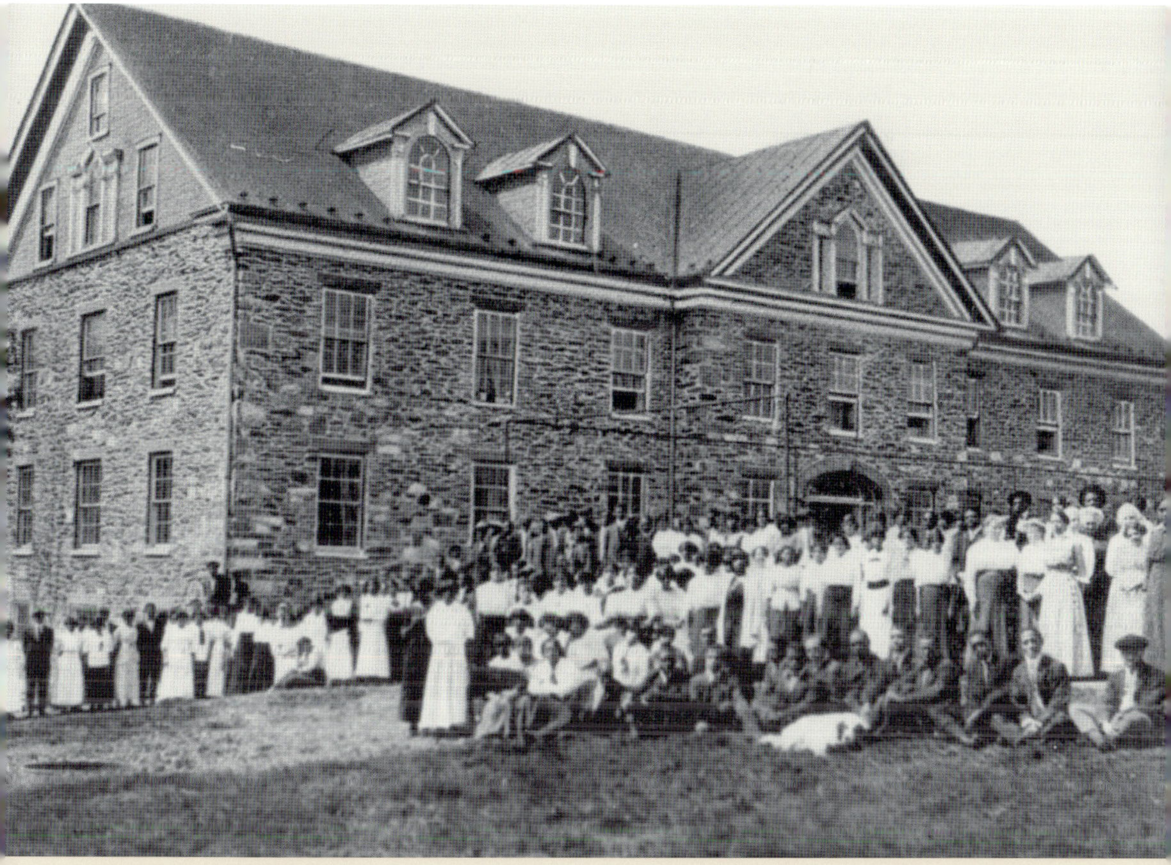

A generous contribution from John Storer helped to establish a school to teach freedmen (former slaves) in Harpers Ferry. Storer Normal College opened its doors on October 2, 1867. The school was open to anyone without regard for race, religion, or sex. Five years later, the school graduated its first class, a total of eight students who could teach in freedmen's schools.

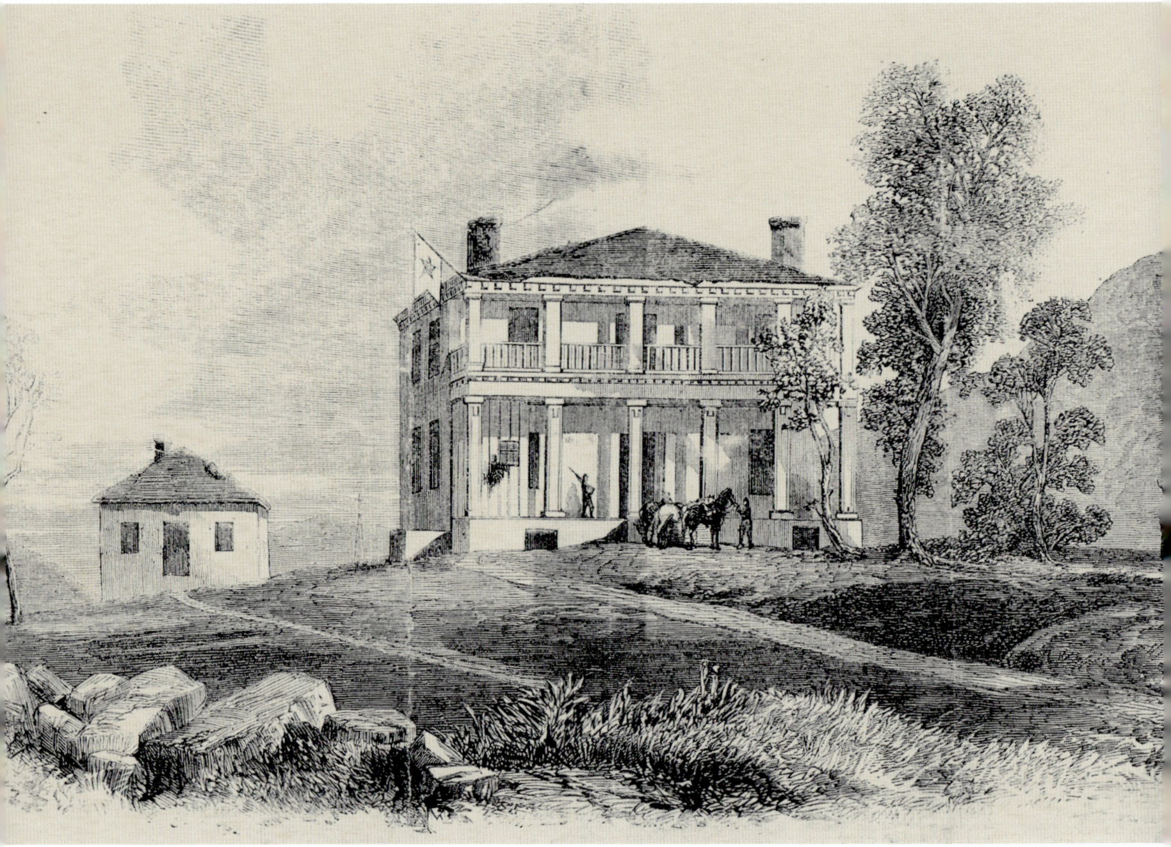

This sketch of Sheridan's headquarters was completed around 1864. Built from 1847 to 1848, it served as the armory paymaster's quarters and had only one story. Second and third stories were added later, with the third story eventually being removed. The "now" photograph shows a fastidiously restored building on the grounds of what used to be the Storer College campus. Today the National Park Service uses the building for offices.

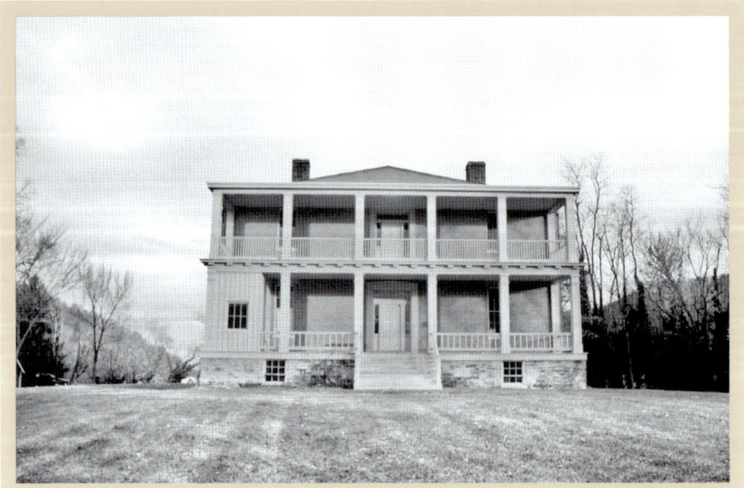

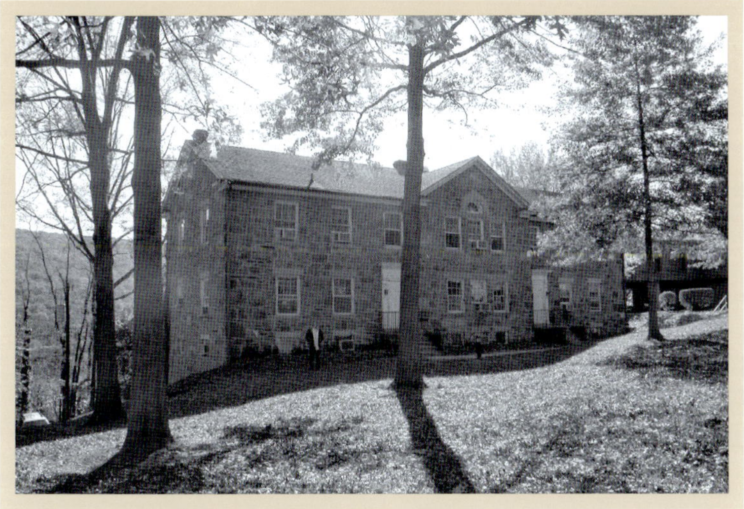

It was 1940 when this building, the Permella Eastman Cook Hall, was constructed. It served as a home economics building as well as housing a physics laboratory. The "now" photograph shows the building restored. Today the building is used as a dormitory for visiting park service workers. In order to be admitted to Storer College, the students were required to give evidence of good moral character. It usually took students three years to complete the course of study.

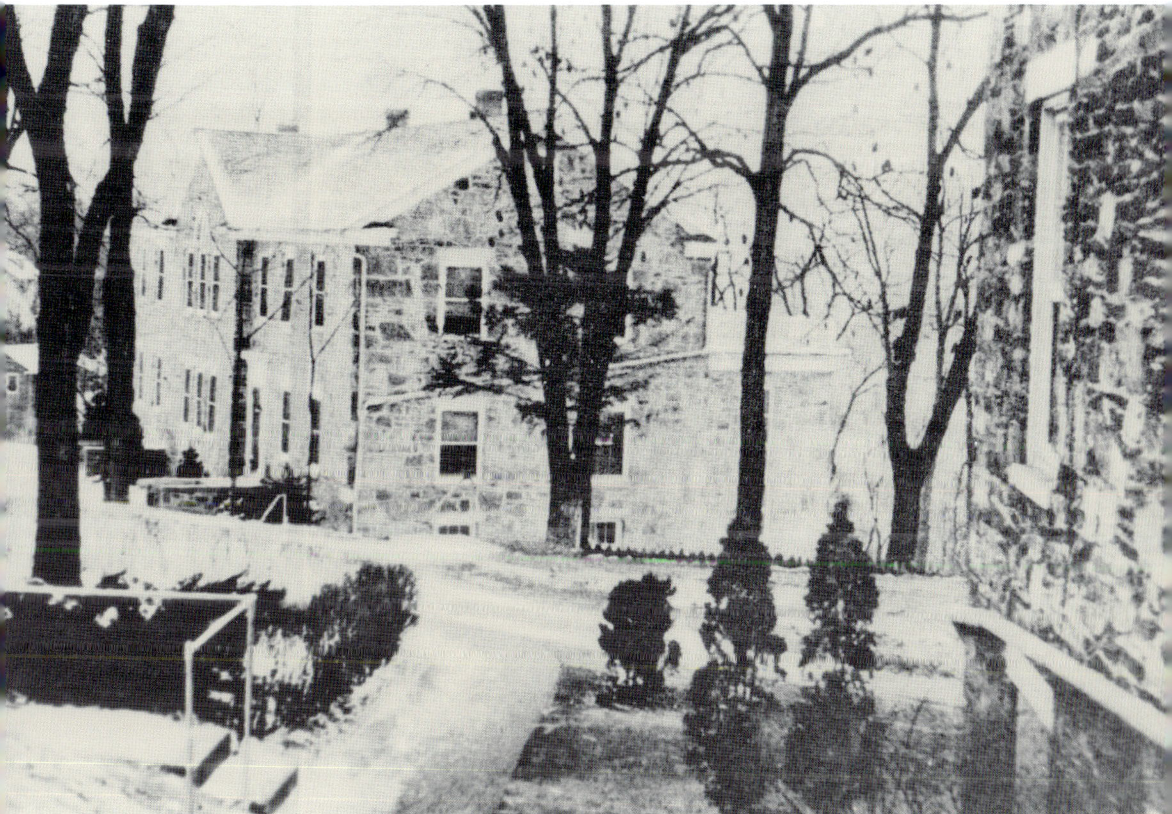

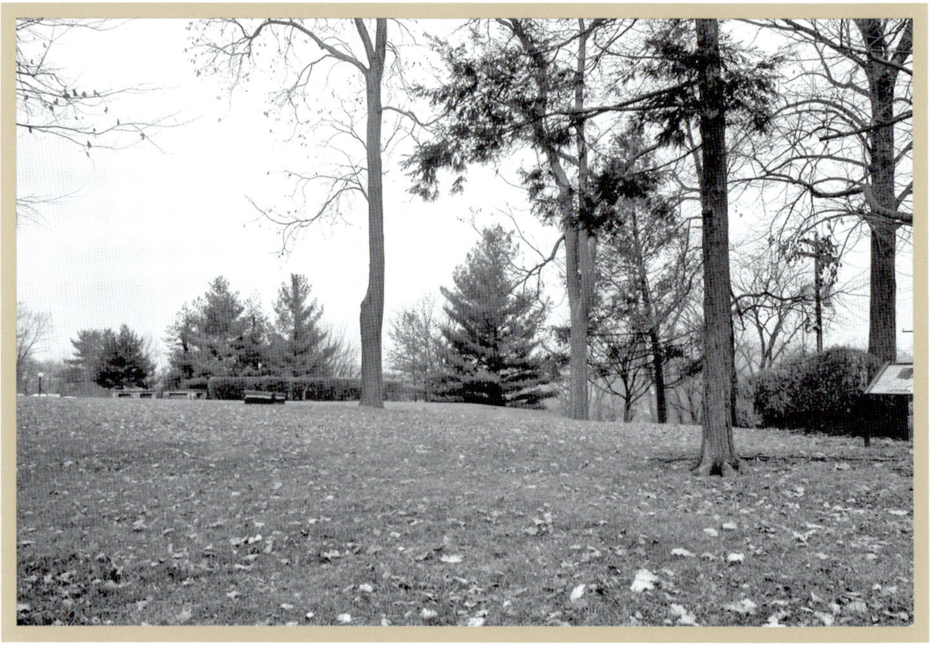

Myrtle Hall is seen in this *c.* 1905 photograph. It was completed in 1879 and served as a dormitory. There were 35 rooms for 60 women as well as several teachers. It was named after *The Myrtle*, the school newspaper. The "now" photograph shows lush green grass where Myrtle Hall once stood. It was torn down in 1962.

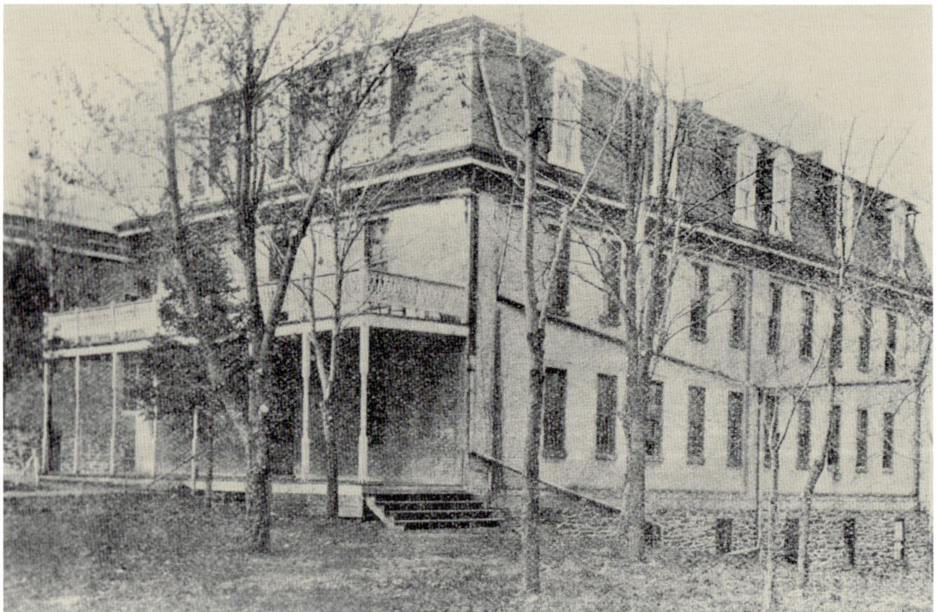

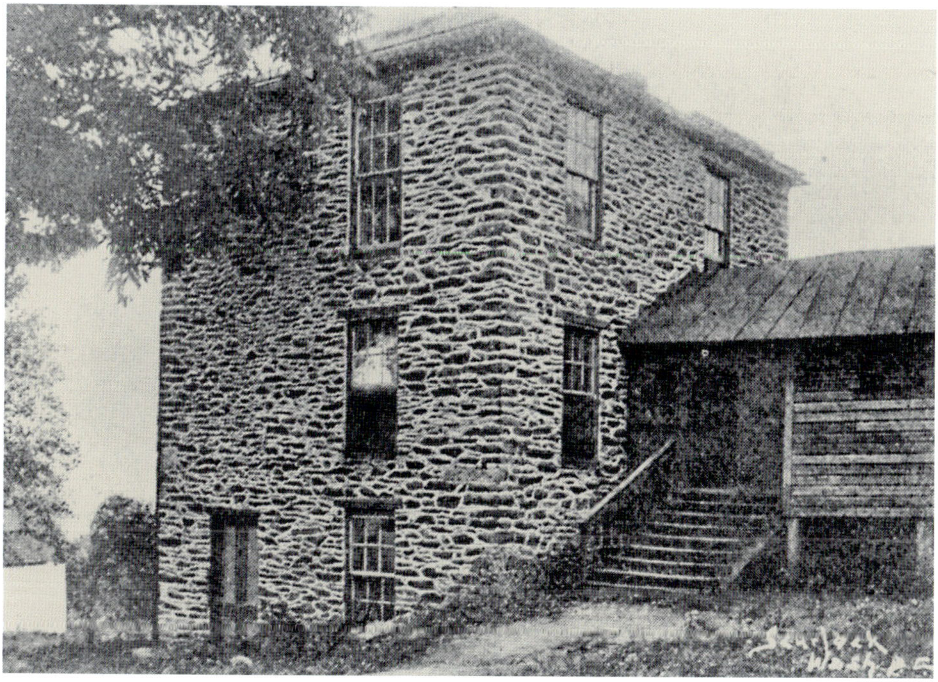

The "then" photograph shows the stone three-story De Wolf Industrial Building, which was erected in 1891. It was demolished in 1947 but housed many things. Here were located botany classes and a physical science lab. Also in this building was a demonstration kitchen. In the "now" photograph, the site where the De Wolf building stood is directly behind Anthony Hall.

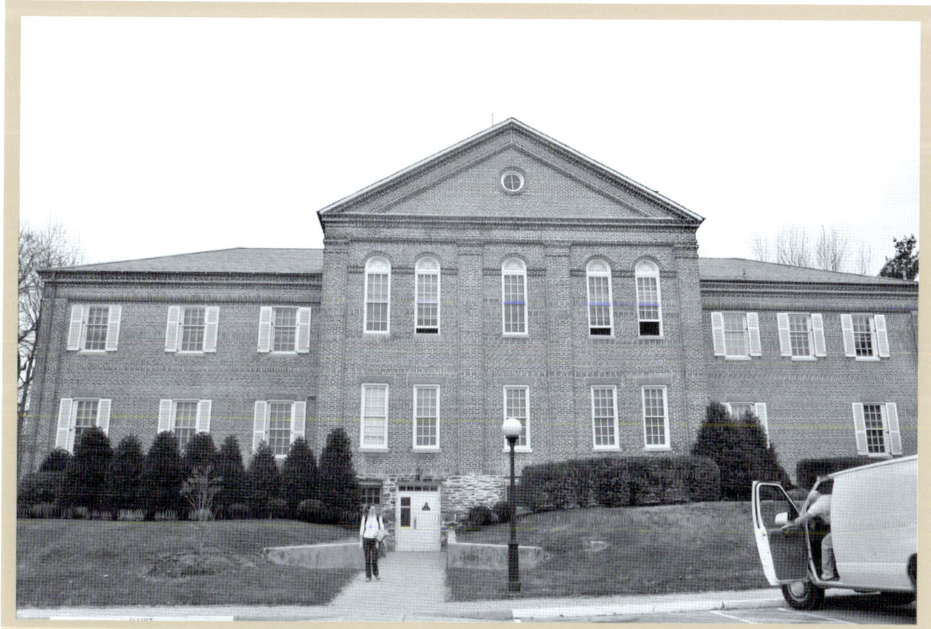

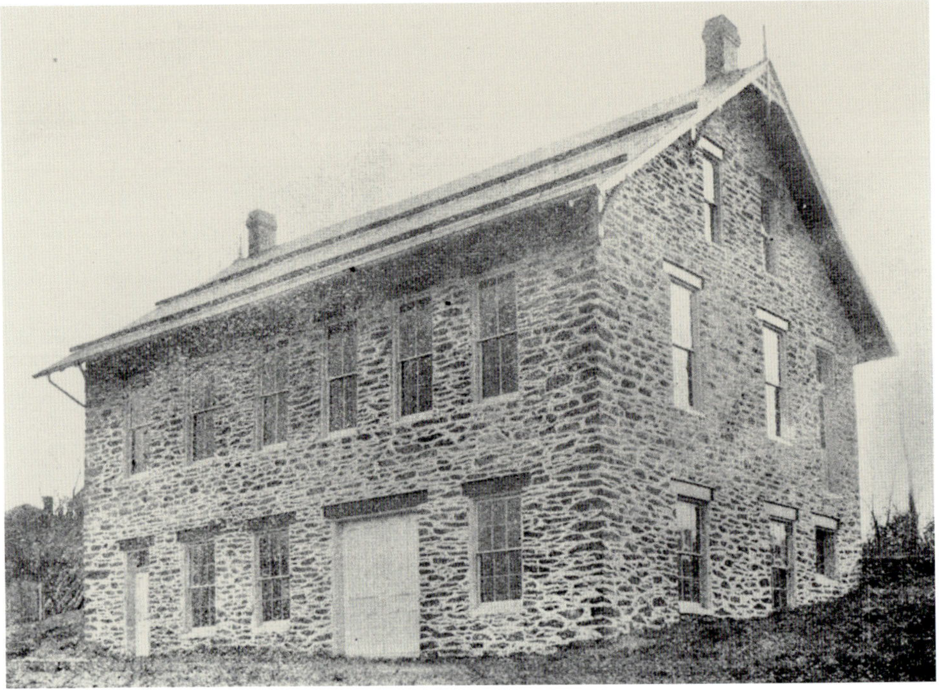

The "now" photograph of the Lewis W. Anthony Industrial Building shows that an addition has been constructed onto the back of the original building. Originally the building had a blacksmith shop, office, storeroom, and carpenter shop. It was erected in 1903. The "then" photograph shows the stone building to be in good shape. Today the building is used as a library, having been converted to such in 1929.

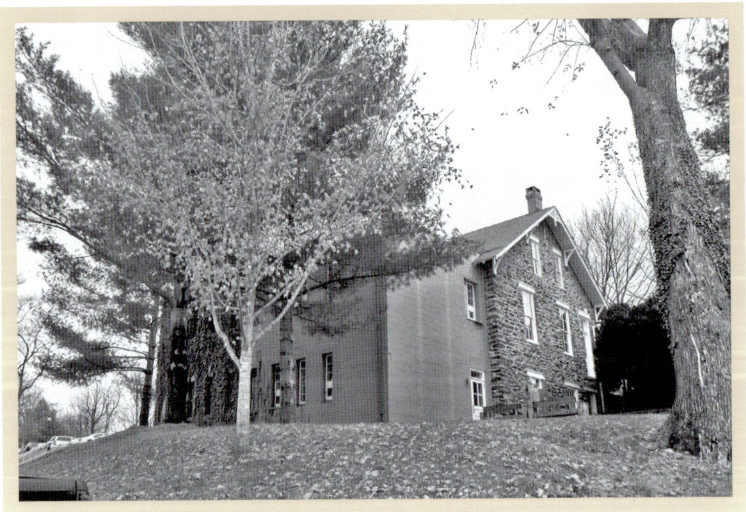

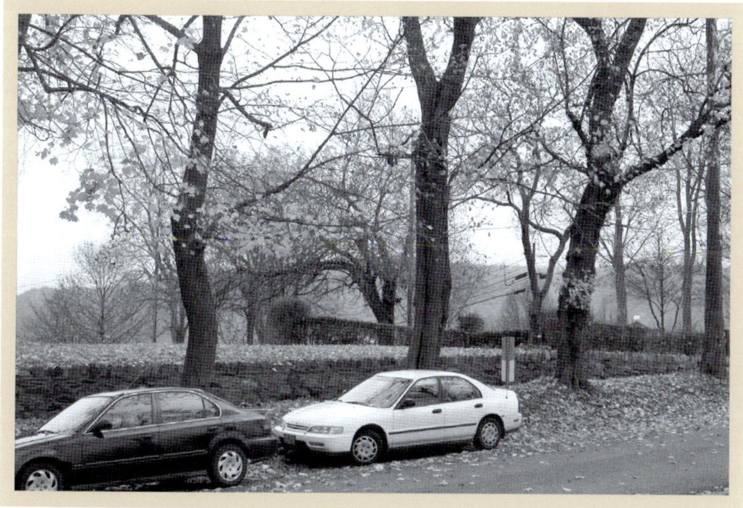

The lot that formerly held the president's house is located on the west end of Fillmore Street. It was also called Sinclair Cottage. The "then" photograph appeared in the 1911–1912 Storer College catalog. The "now" photograph shows an empty lot. Between 1912 and 1923, the college purchased several small cottages to house both teachers and students. In 1962, the National Park Service demolished most of them.

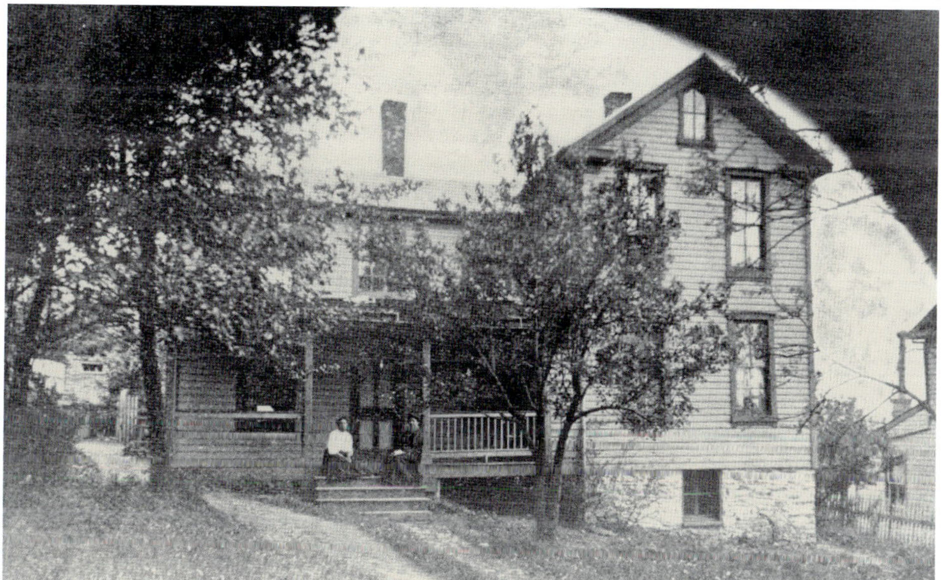

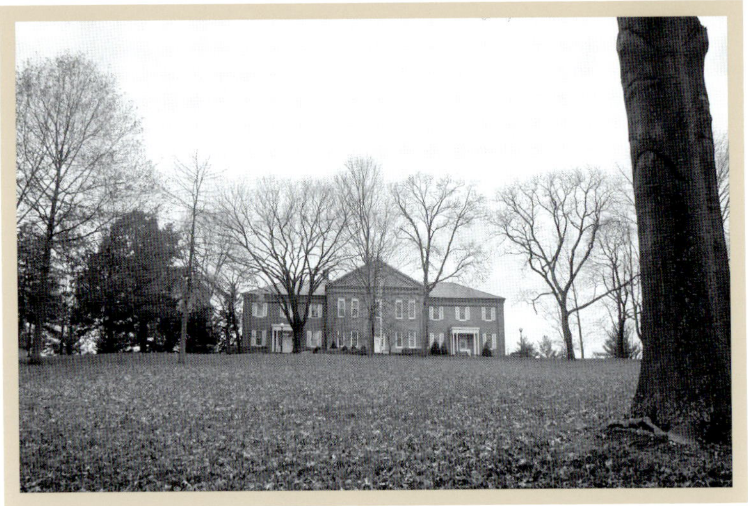

October 24, 1927, witnessed the burning of Anthony Hall. It had been built between 1847 and 1848, and it served as the armory superintendent's house. President Lincoln was an overnight guest in the hall on October 1, 1862. When Storer College opened, the building was donated to the trustees of the college. It was named after Lewis W. Anthony in gratitude for his donations. After the fire in 1927, it was rebuilt in 1928 on top of the old foundation. Today it houses the Mather Training Center, an educational facility for park employees.

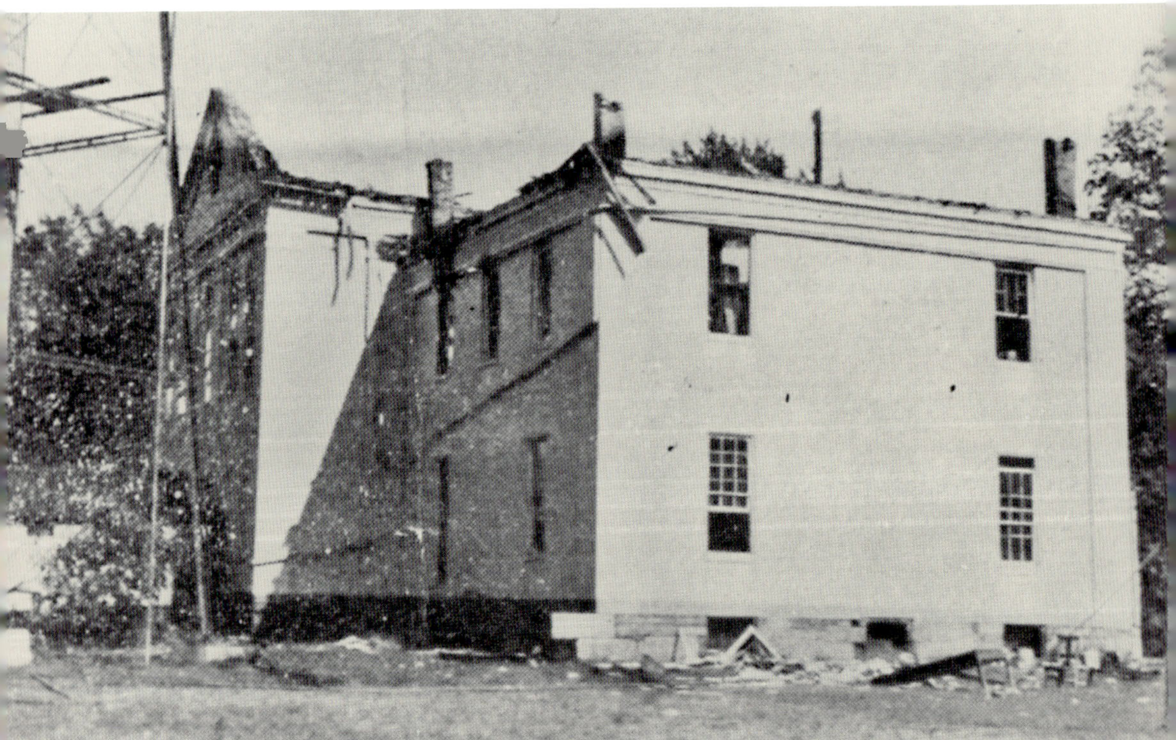

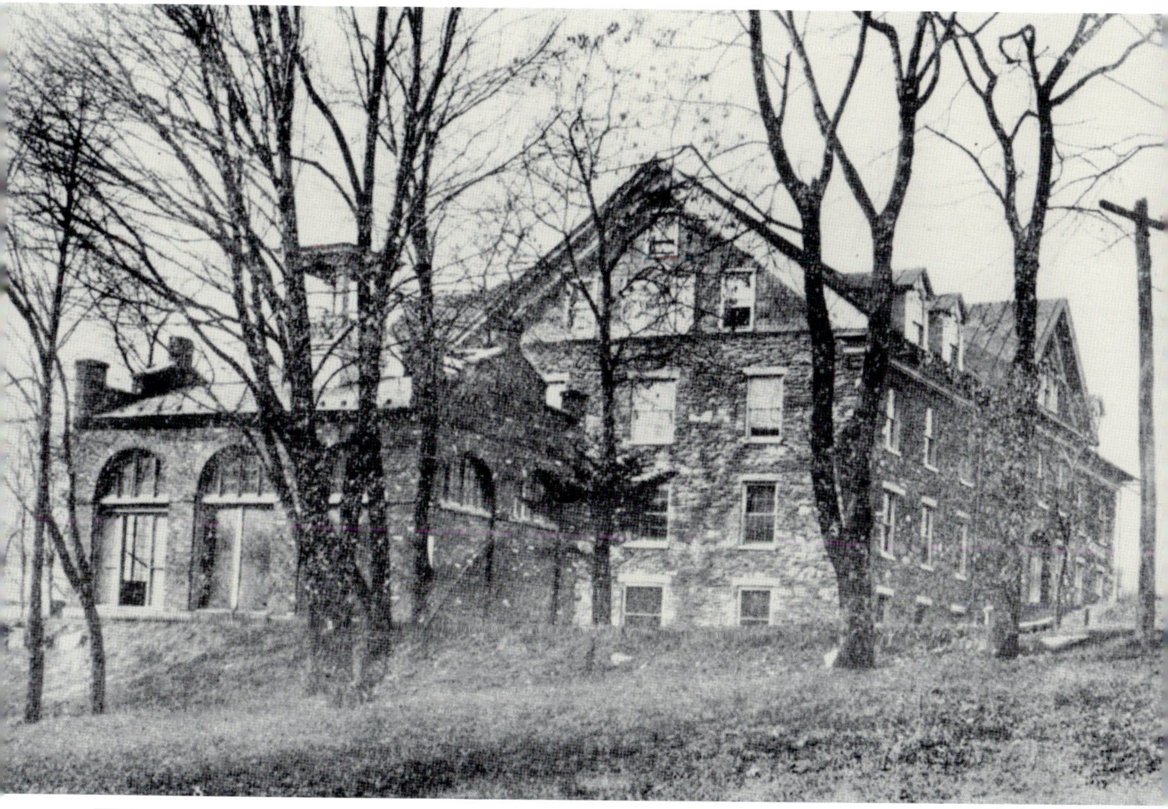

Lincoln Hall, the boys' dormitory, had been constructed between 1870 and 1871 and contained 34 double rooms. On April 12, 1909, the three-story building burned down. It was rebuilt and renamed Brackett Hall in 1938. In Brackett Hall were a flat for the superintendent, a YMCA room, a kitchen and accompanying dining room for the men's club, a gymnasium, and a general reception area. In 1962, it was demolished, and the National Park Service's Interpretive Design Center is located there today.

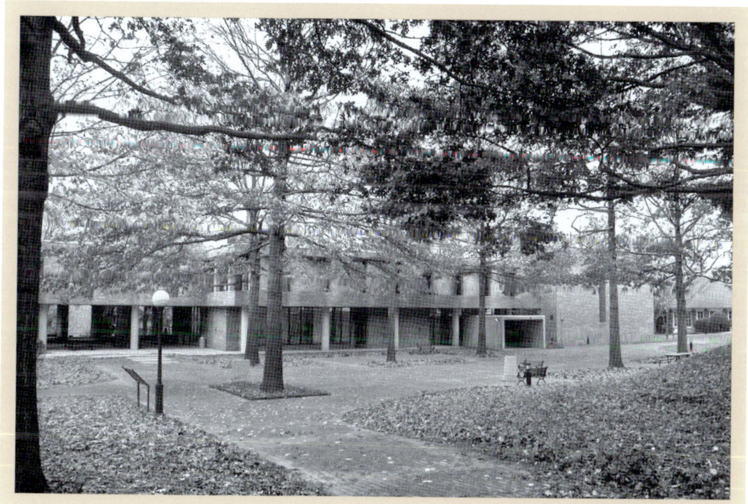

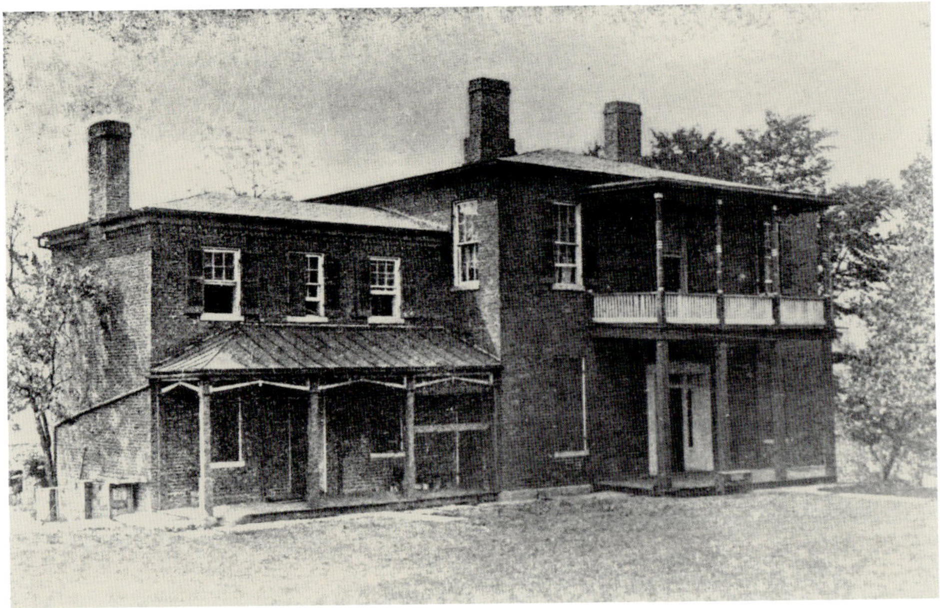

The Brackett House was built in 1858 and was originally known as Building No. 31. The house was conveyed to Storer College in December 1869. Both students and teachers were provided with housing in this building for more than 80 years. It was named after Dr. Nathan Cook Brackett, who was instrumental in the founding of the college. The "then" photograph was taken around 1908. The "now" photograph shows that the building has been restored.

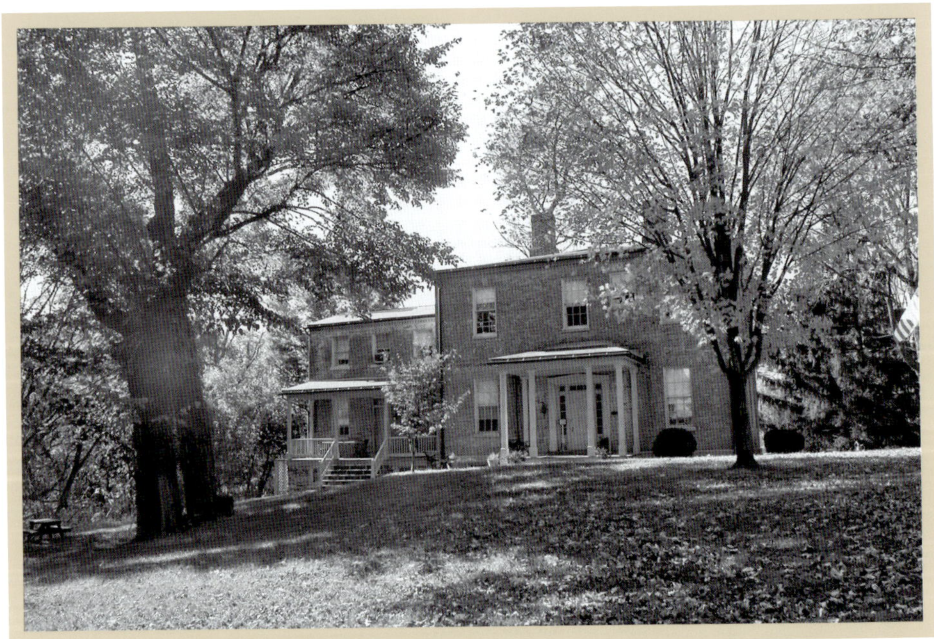

CHAPTER 5

H_2O AND SPANS

SHENANDOAH AND POTOMAC RIVERS AND BRIDGES

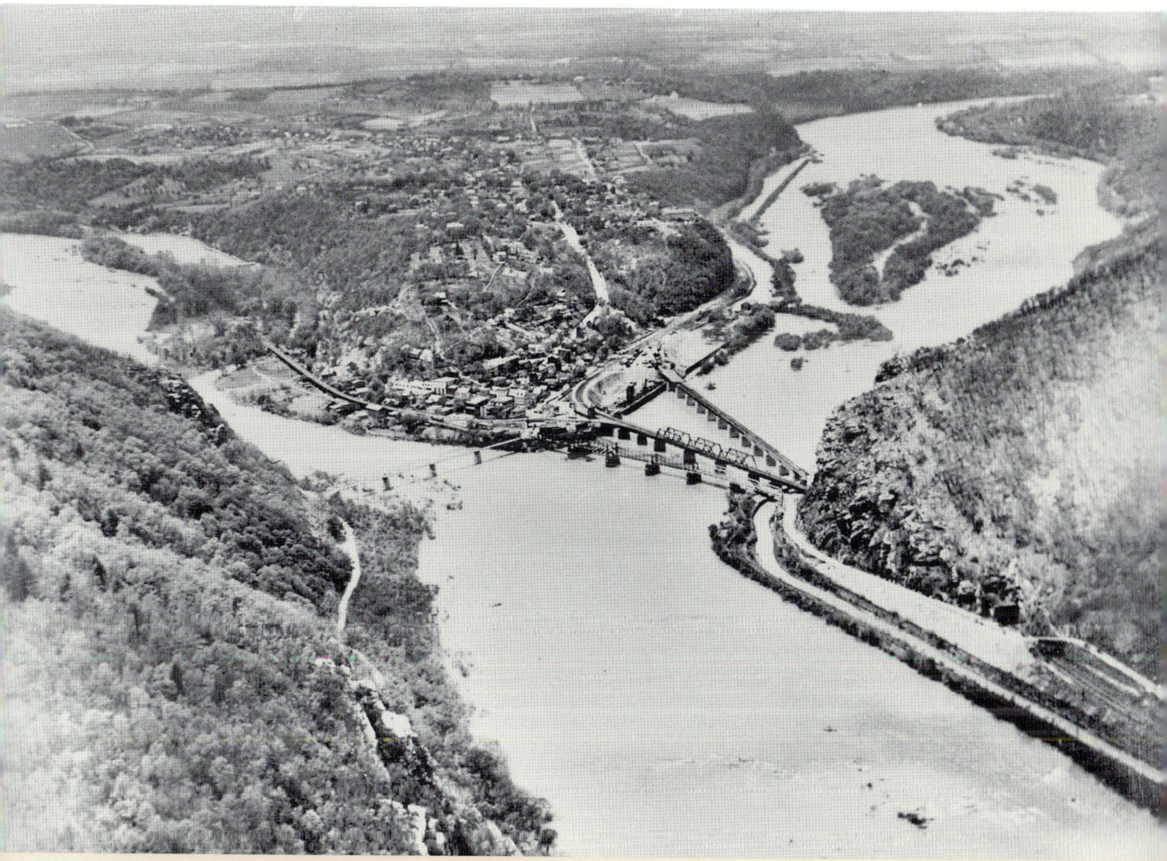

This photograph was taken in 1932, when the water level was elevated during a flood, and clearly shows the many islands along both the Potomac and the Shenandoah Rivers. To the right, the Potomac River and Byrne's Island are easily identified. To the left, jutting into the Shenandoah River, is Virginius Island. Also visible on the left is Lake Quigley. All of the bridges are still intact—floods such as pictured here would destroy or damage many.

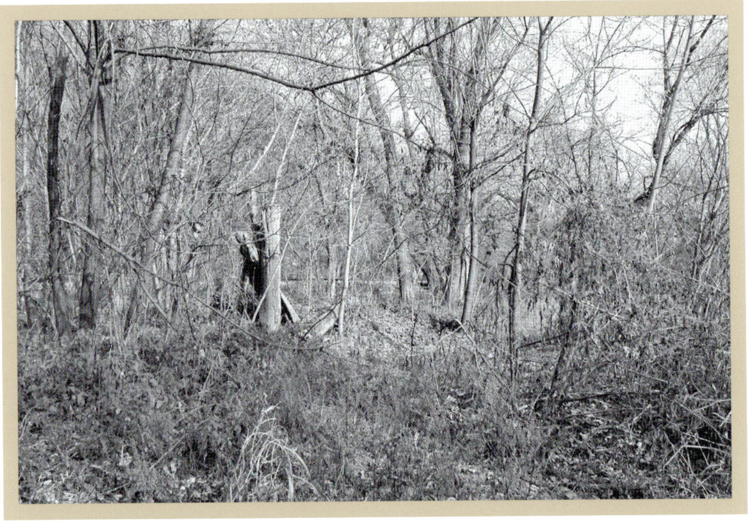

Pictured in the "then" photograph is what appears to be a dwelling place built for workers on the island. An island entrepreneur or owner likely resided in this house. Other dwellings were also constructed on the island to house workers and included 5 two-story brick tenements, 5 half-story wooden cottages, and 4 large two-story structures. All that remains today are skeletal foundations.

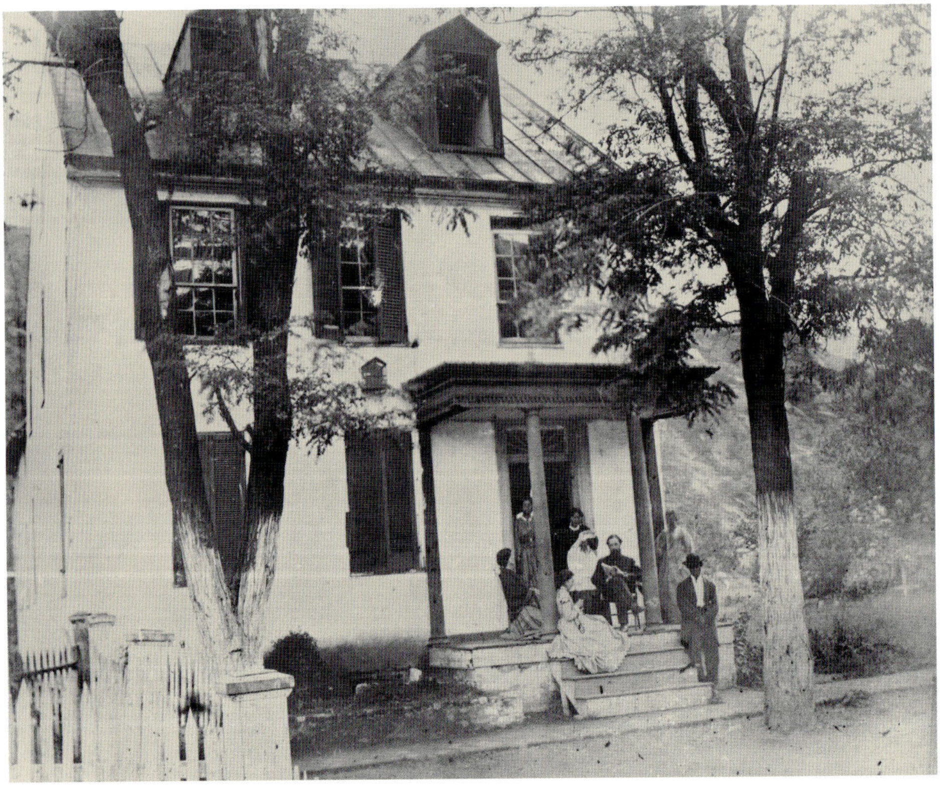

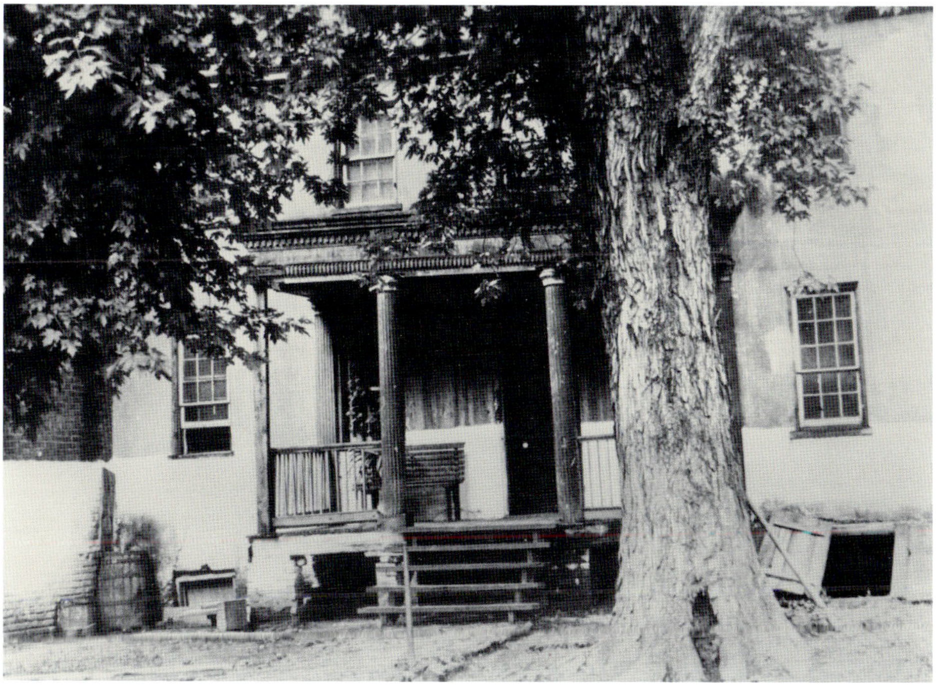

The "then" photograph shows the Jonathan Child House on Virginius Island. In 1867, Jonathan C. Child and John McCreight purchased holdings from Abraham Herr, after which they converted the old cotton factory into a flour mill. The family moved into this house the same year. Thanks to the research conducted by the National Park Service, the location of the house could be found for the "now" photograph, although not much detail is visible.

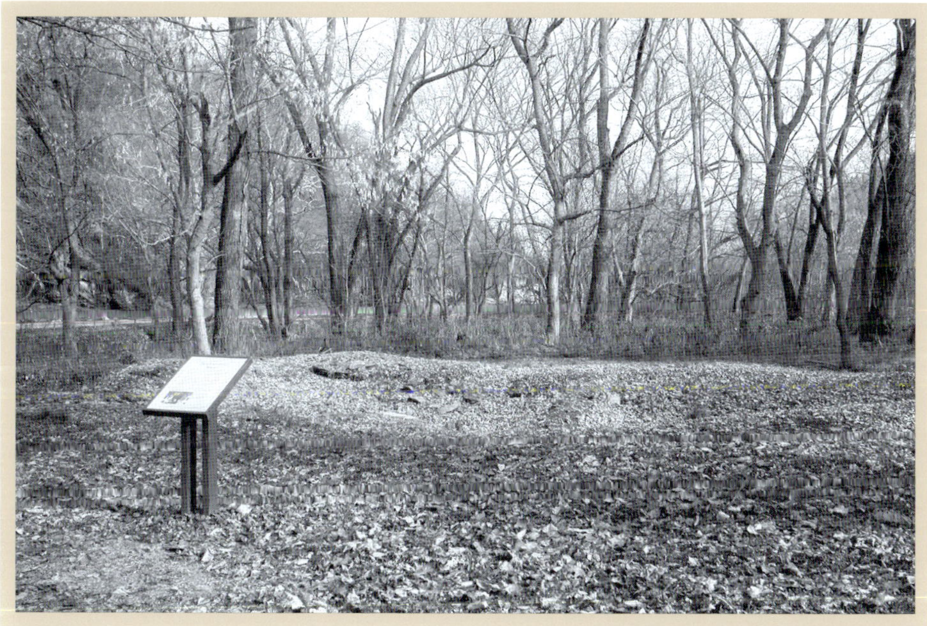

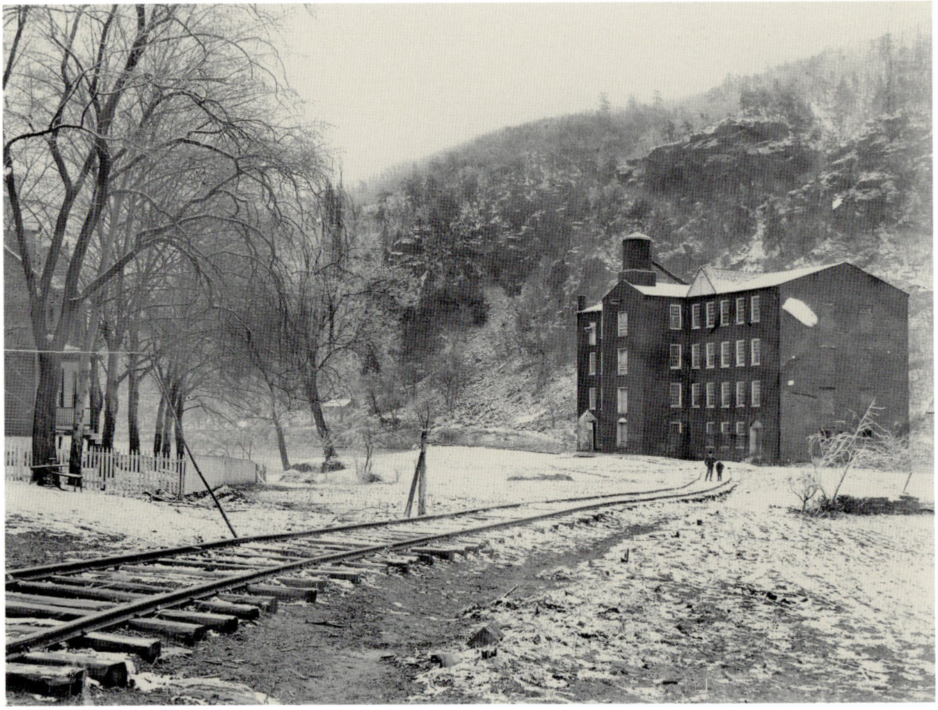

In the "then" photograph, the Child and McCreight Mill is shown. Prior to being converted to a flour mill that produced 80,000 barrels a year, this was a cotton factory. Built in 1848, the four-story building was located on Virginius Island on the banks of the Shenandoah, which provided waterpower for the machines. Today all that is visible is the skeletal foundation of the once-prosperous factory. Its many uses included a cotton factory (1848–1852), a Union hospital (1863–1865), and a flour mill (1867–1889).

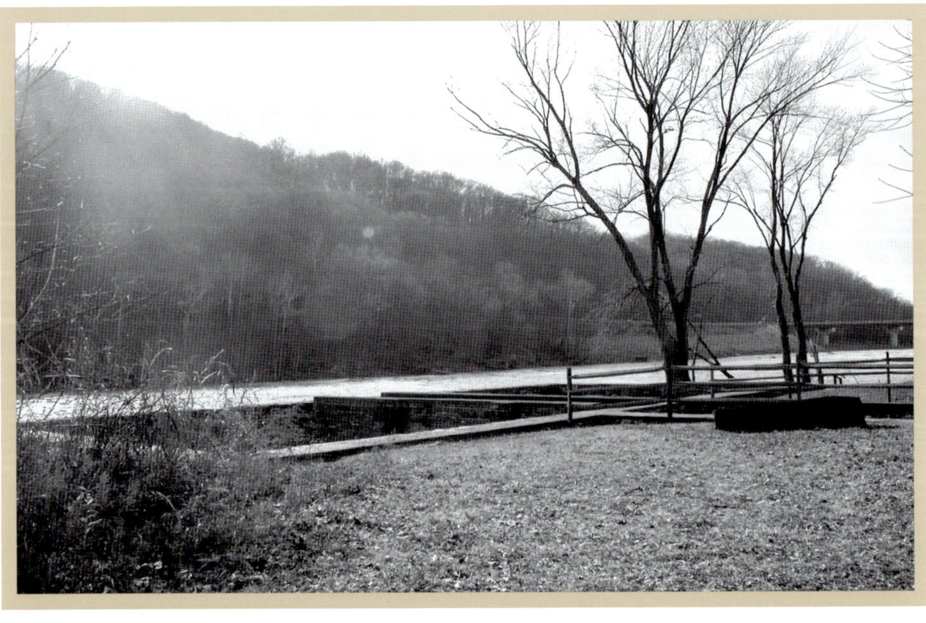

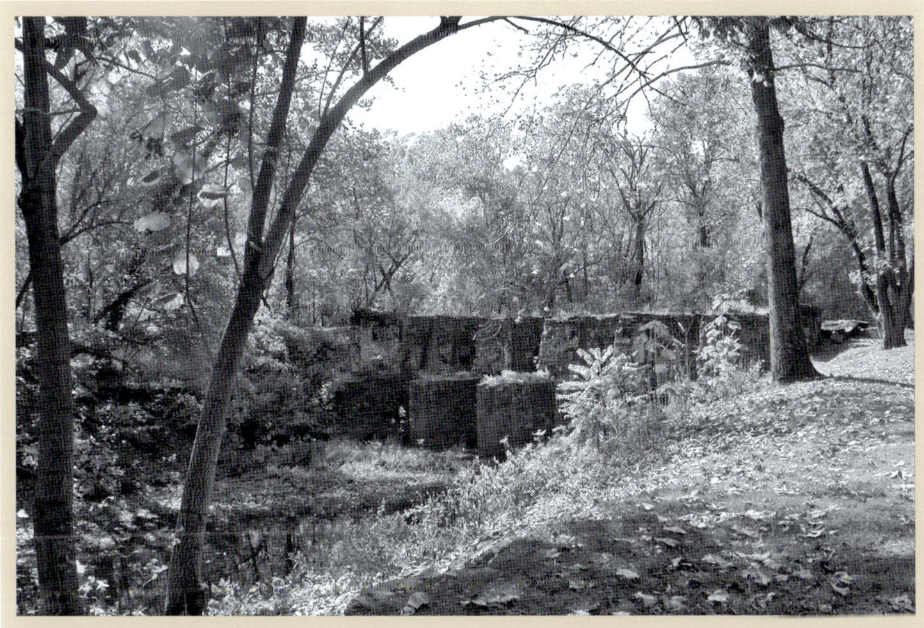

The Shenandoah Pulp Mill, located on the banks of Lake Quigley, opened in 1888 and remained in operation until 1935. The "now" photograph shows all that remains of the mill today. It was equipped with 10 turbines that produced more than 2,300 horsepower. Although its peak capacity was 40 tons of wood pulp daily, by 1927, it was producing just 15 tons daily. The company was liquidated in 1936, and the State of West Virginia dissolved the corporation on June 25 of that year.

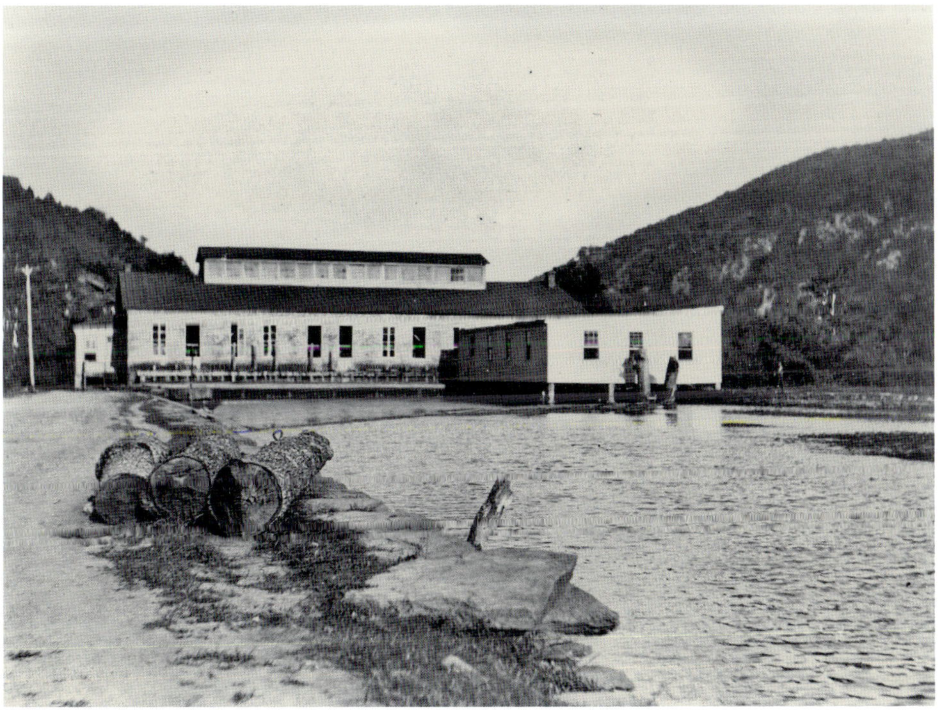

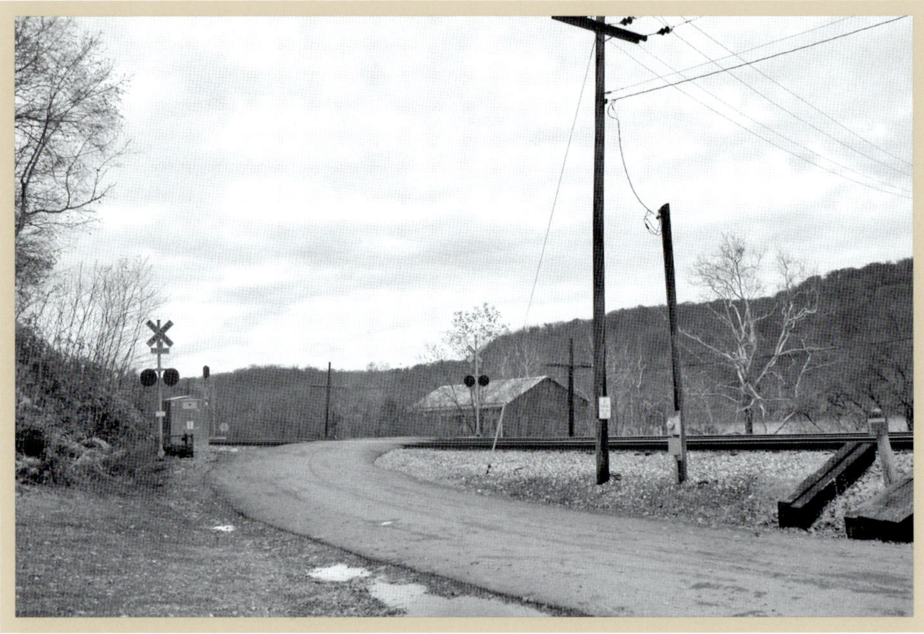

Prior to being used as a power company, this building housed the Harpers Ferry Paper Company. It burned on January 15, 1925, and the remnant walls were incorporated into the power company building. The paper company had been owned by members of the Savery family, and after the fire, they designed the plant to generate hydroelectricity exclusively. The new walls were constructed from recycled bricks from the Child and McCreight flour mill.

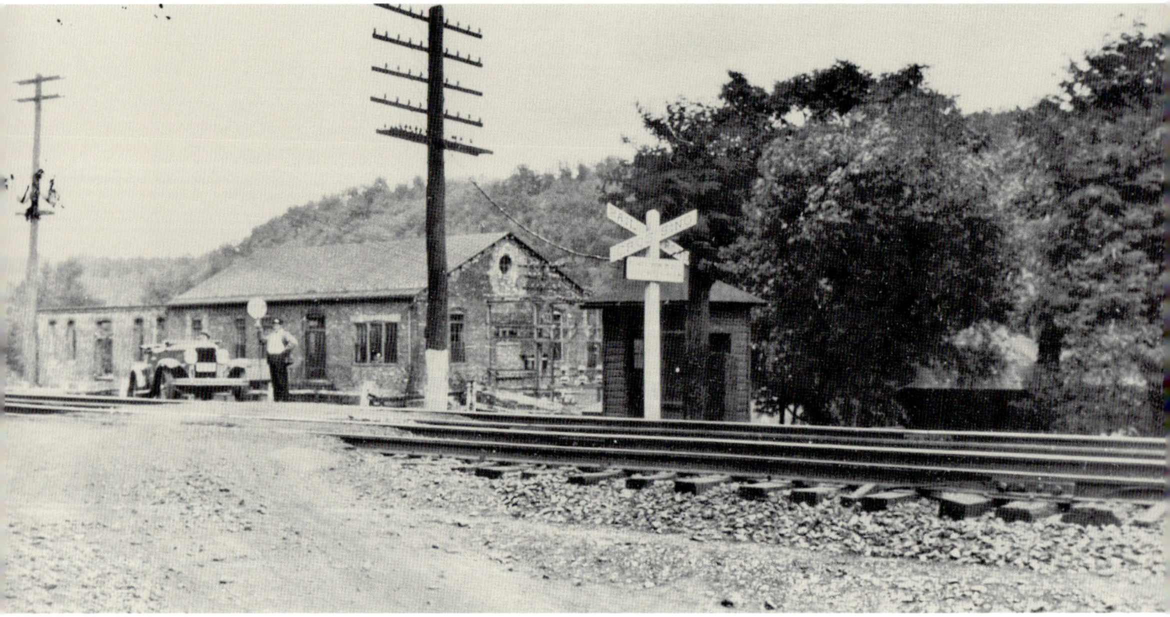

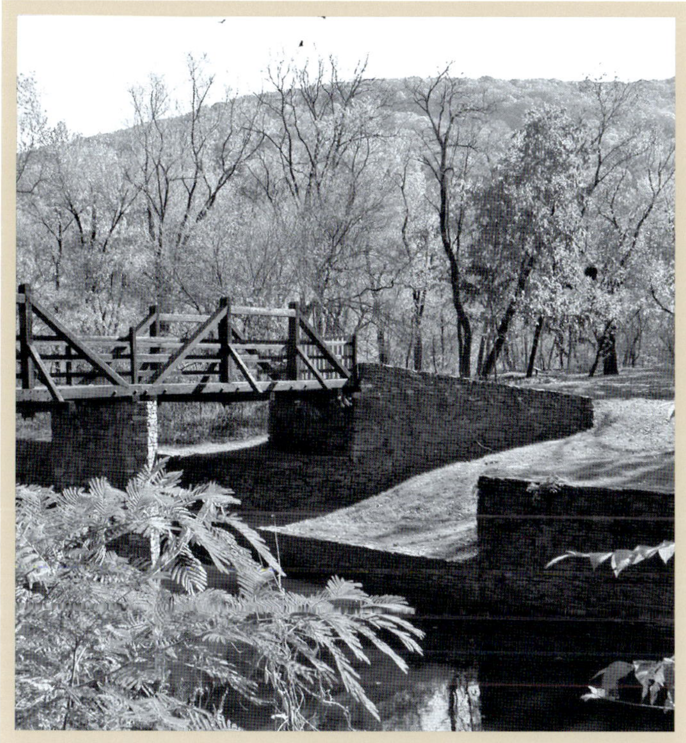

Access to Virginius Island from the mainland was accomplished by bridges. The wooden truss bridge in this "then" photograph leads to the island. The road then went past houses and possibly a factory as well. In addition, there appears to be a road going into the raceway. The "now" photograph shows a reproduction of the wooden truss bridge, which was dedicated to former West Virginia U.S. Sen. Jennings Randolph as gratitude for his efforts to establish Harpers Ferry as a national historical park.

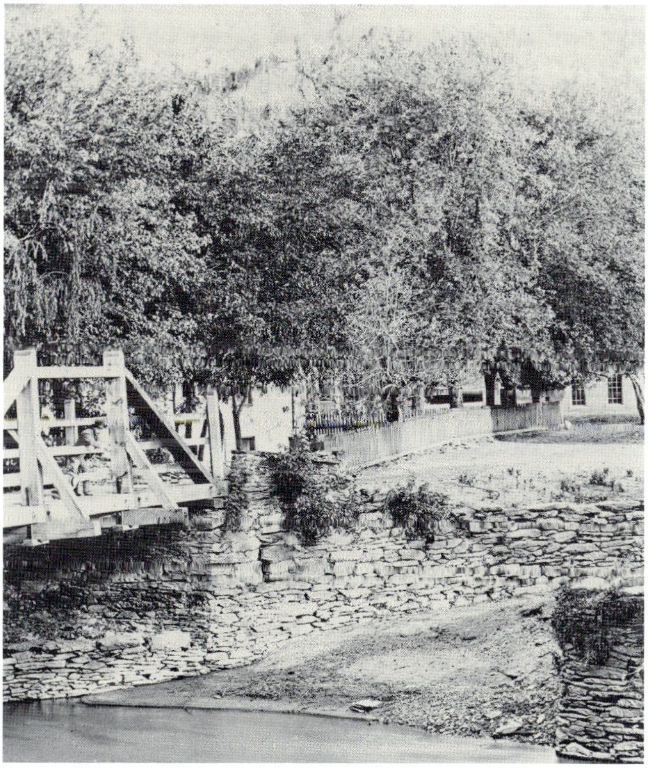

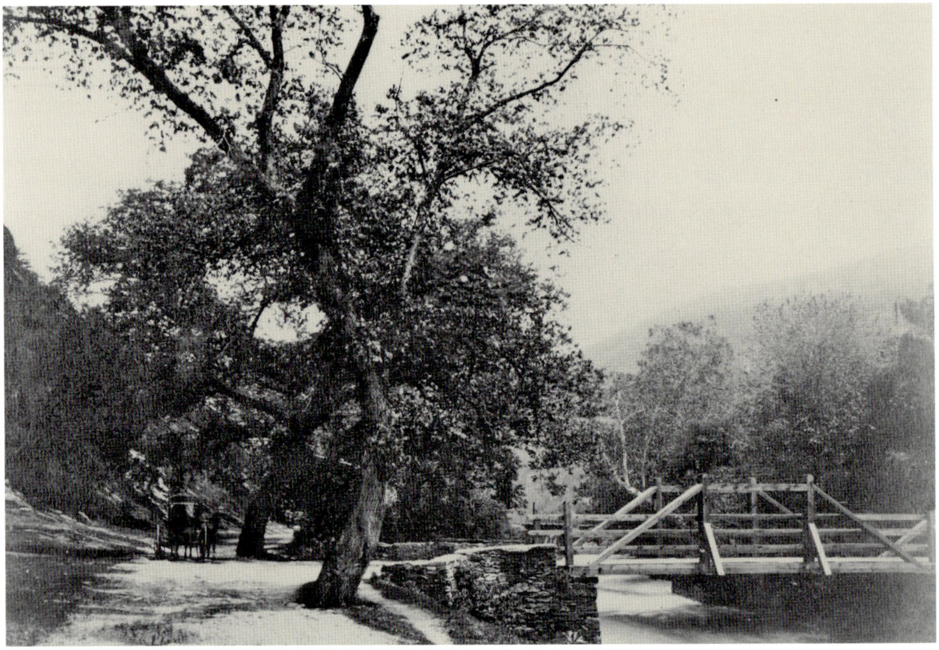

In this "then" photograph, a horse and buggy can be seen ambling along Shenandoah Street. To the right is a wooden truss bridge leading to Virginius Island. It was a photograph such as this that park service personnel used to reconstruct the wooden truss bridge in the "now" photograph. From time to time, the bridge is closed when repairs are being completed to the island or to the bridge.

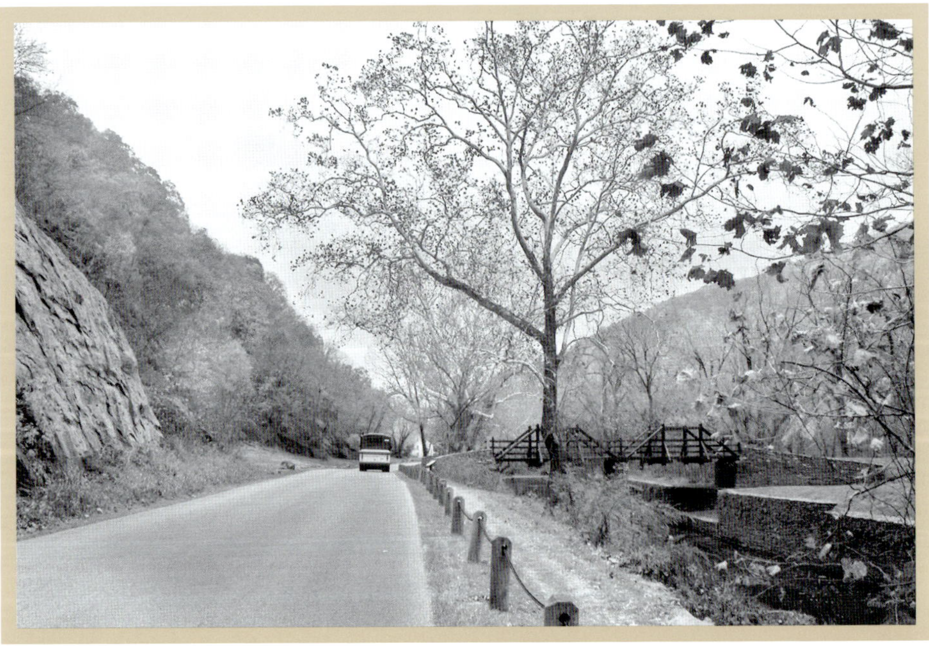

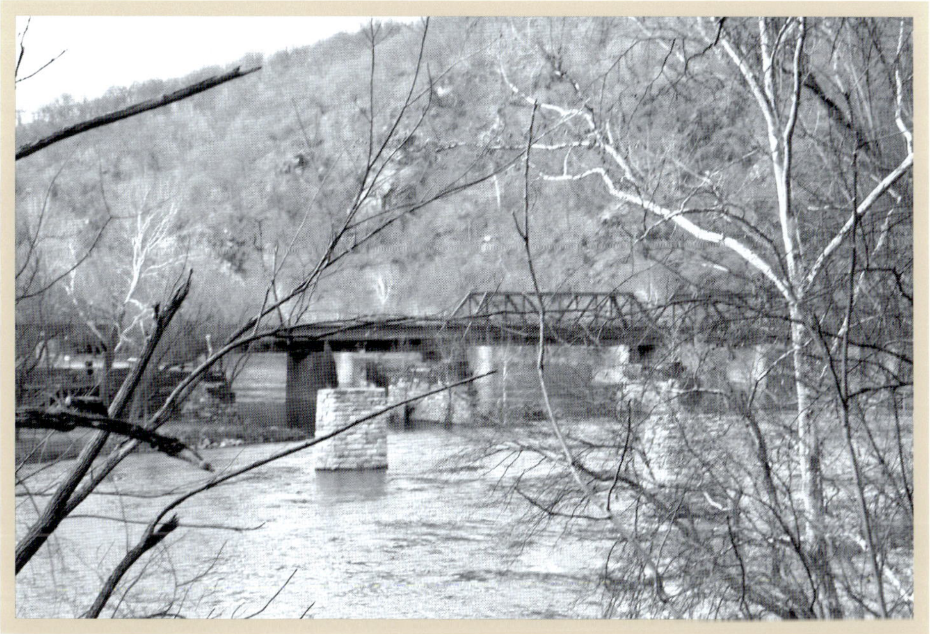

The Shenandoah River bridge in the "then" photograph extended from Lower Town to Loudoun Heights. The railroad bridge extended from Lower Town to Maryland Heights. In the "then" photograph can be seen a horse and buggy approaching Loudoun Heights. Also visible is a horse and buggy in the lower right corner, possibly waiting to cross. Today all that is left of the two bridges are the supports. Floods have taken their toll on Harpers Ferry's bridges over the years.

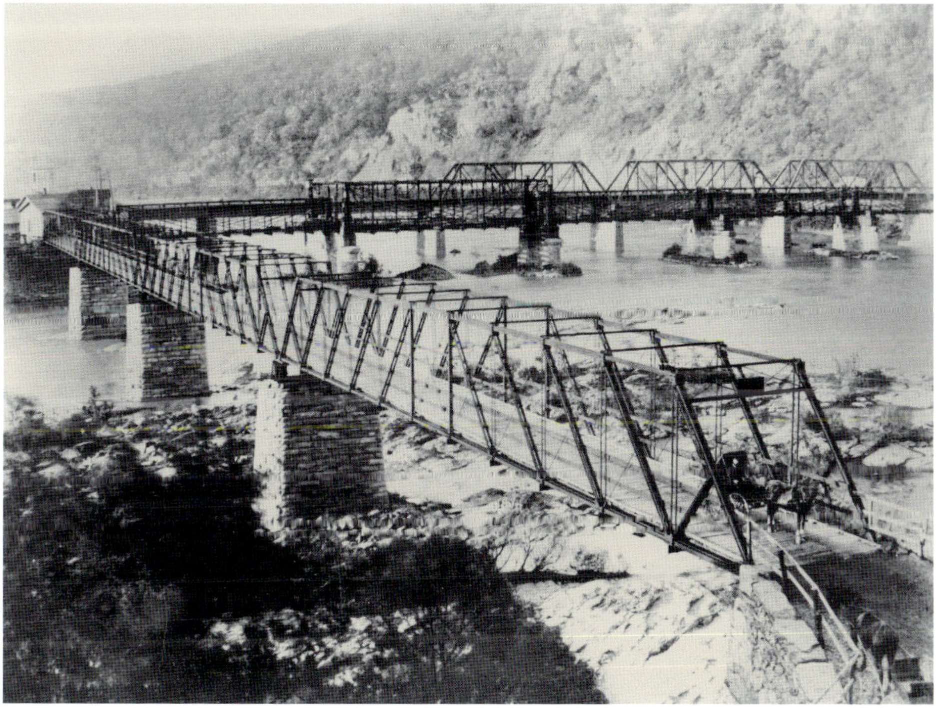

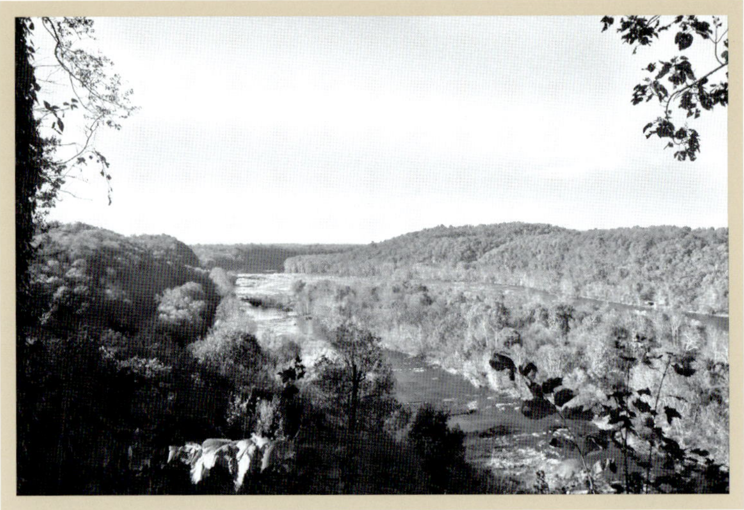

Located on Byrne's Island was an amusement park that the railroad created for its employees. In the "then" photograph can be seen tent-style roofs for the attendees' protection. A pedestrian bridge was provided for crossing the canal. Admittance was free for employees and families. As the "now" photograph shows, the footbridge no longer exists, having been washed away. The island is no longer visited as an amusement park.

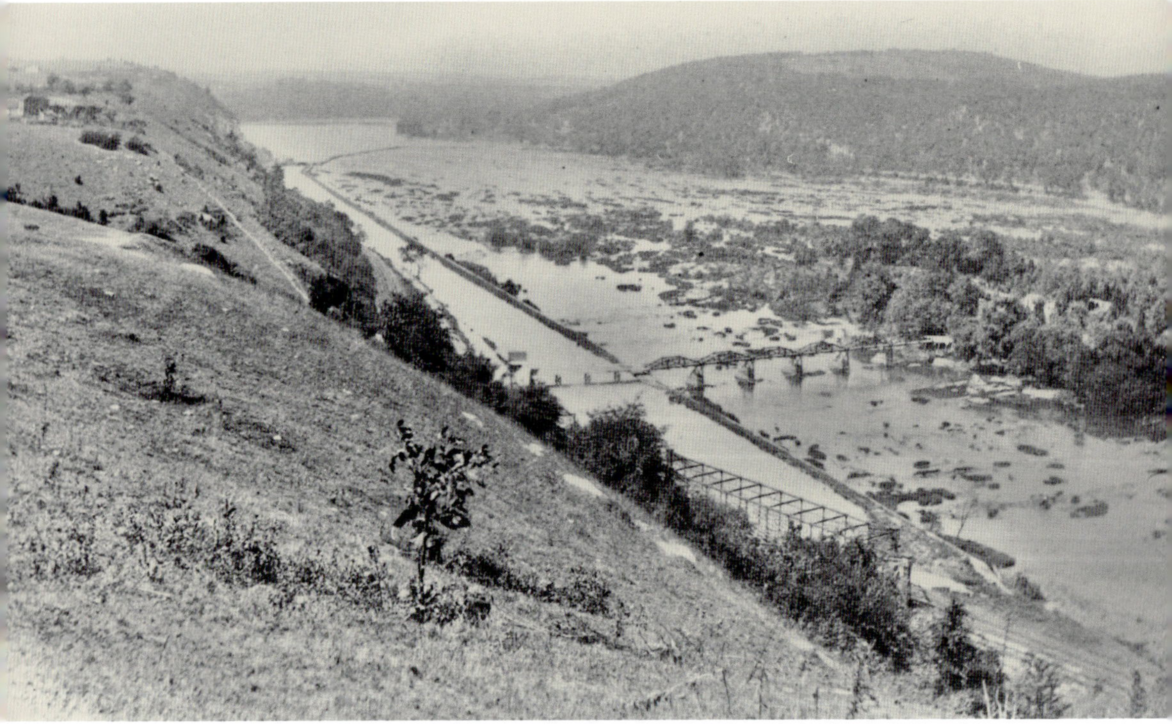

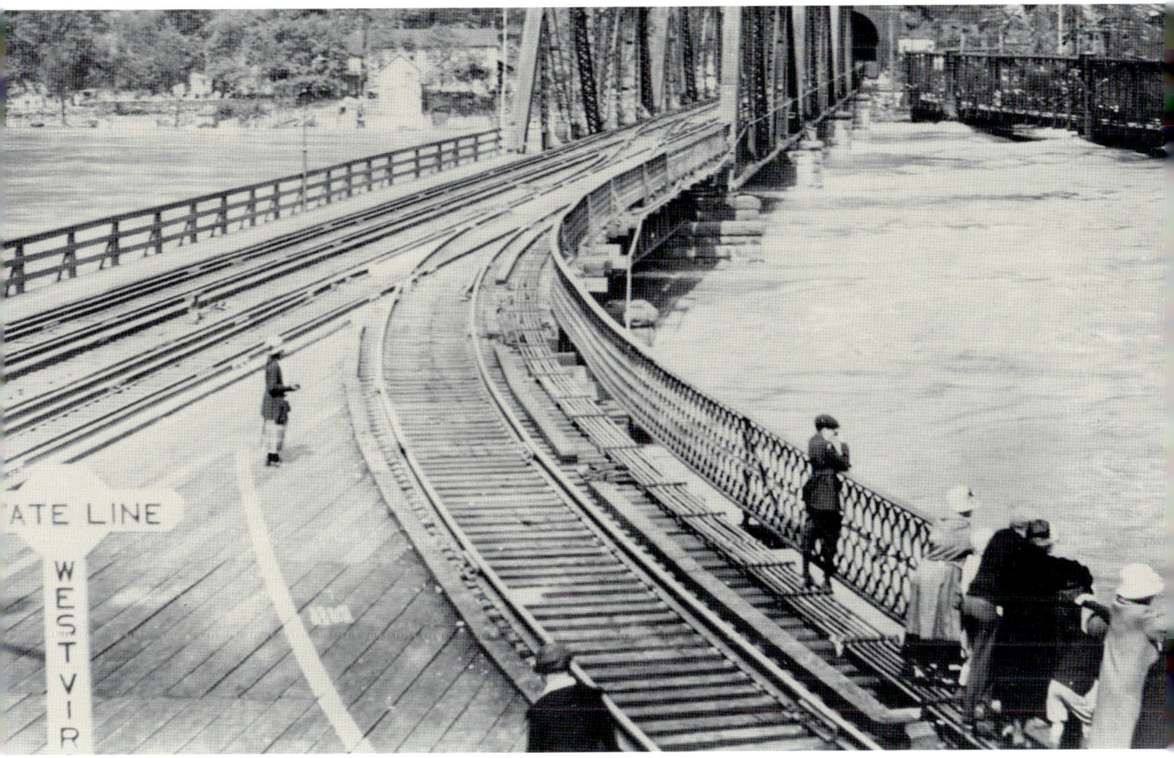

For Harpers Ferry, structurally sound bridges were the key to survival as a community. The "then" photograph was taken during the flood of 1924, and the floodwaters can be seen licking the bottom of the iron bridge. During the 1924 flood, the Lower Town was inundated with pulpwood debris from the Shenandoah Pulp Mill. The "now" photograph was taken from the same vantage point and shows the lower level of the Potomac River.

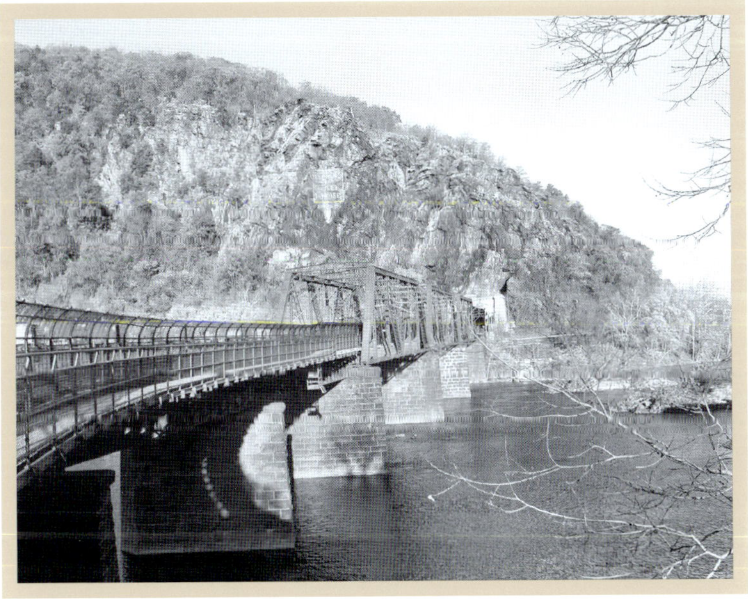

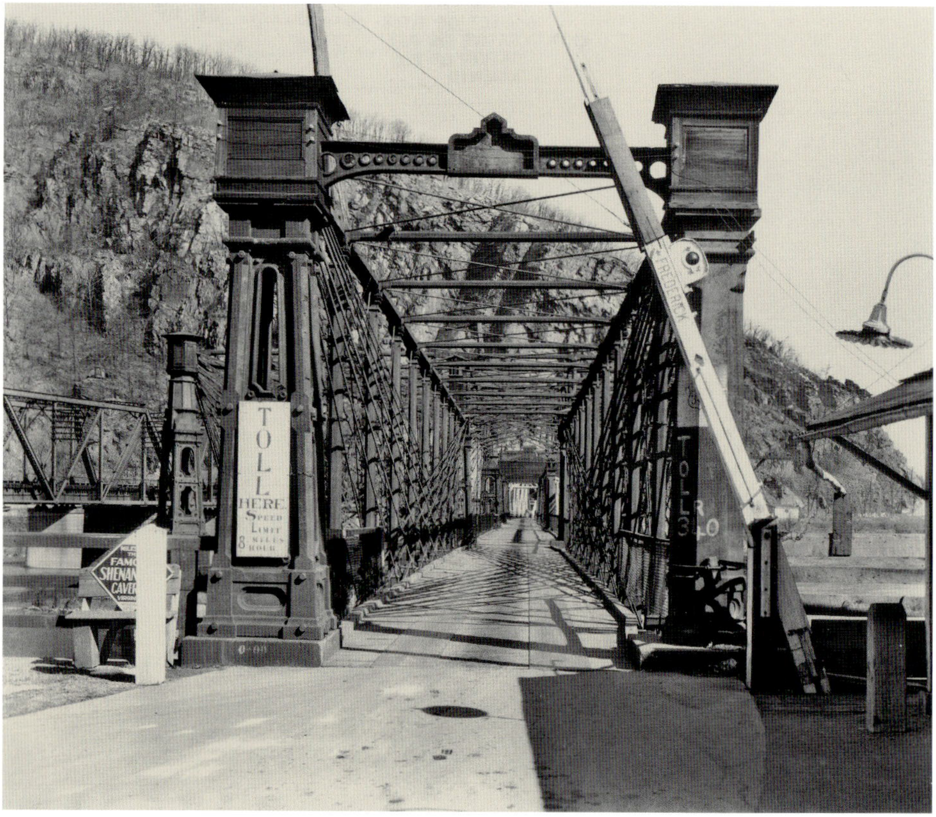

The "then" photograph dates from the 1930s and shows the tollgate on the iron bridge to Maryland Heights. All vehicular traffic was stopped and could not proceed until the toll was paid. The speed limit while driving across the bridge was limited to eight miles per hour. The "now" photograph shows that only trains, and pedestrians behind the fence, can use the bridge. In addition, no tolls are charged.

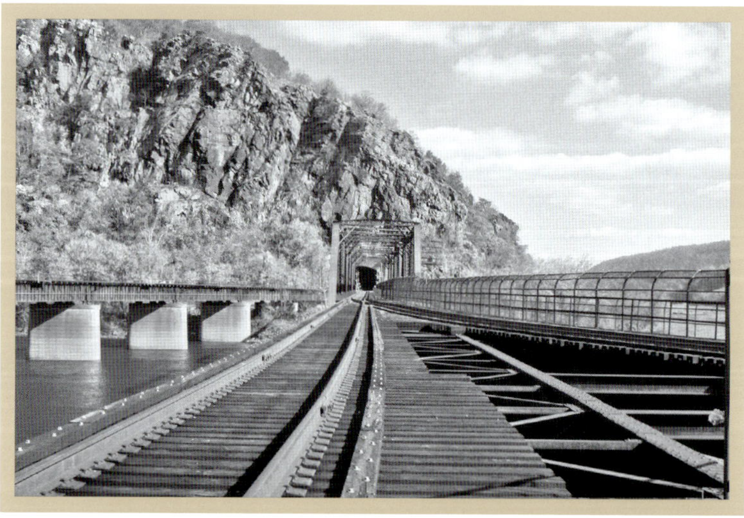

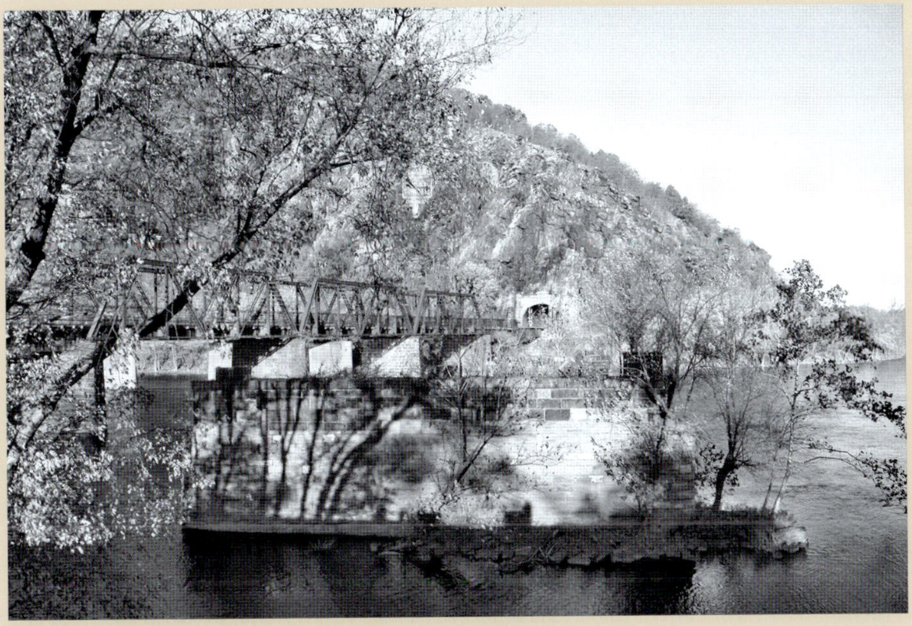

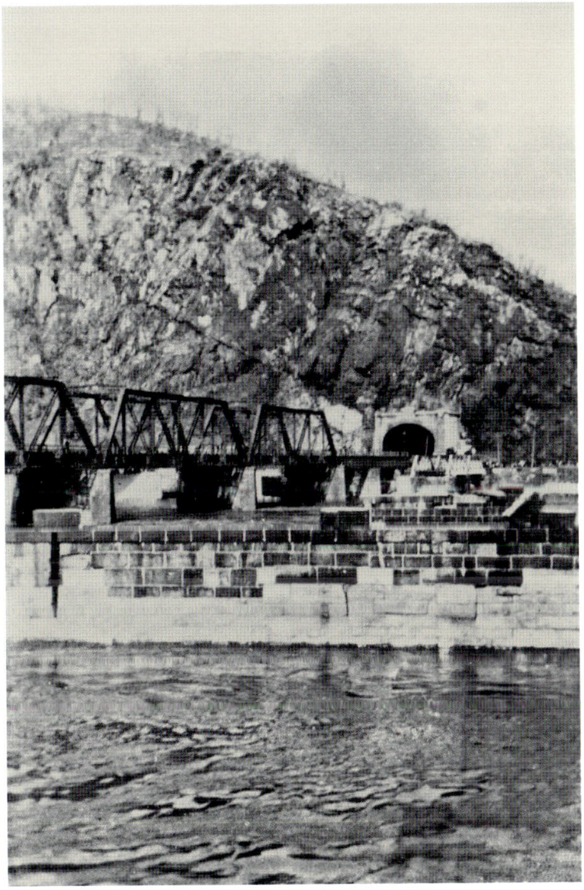

After the devastating flood of 1936, local bridges showed much wear and tear. In this photograph are shown the piers of the 1865 iron bridge, with the water still only four or five feet from the top of the piers. In the photograph of today, one can see that the water level is much lower. Floods in Harpers Ferry took their toll over the years. Memorable floods occurred in 1748, 1753, 1852, 1870, 1877, 1889, 1924, 1936, 1942, 1972, 1985, and twice in 1996. Because of the floods, bridges have needed to be rebuilt many times. The piers show that vegetation will find a place to grow, however unlikely that place might be.

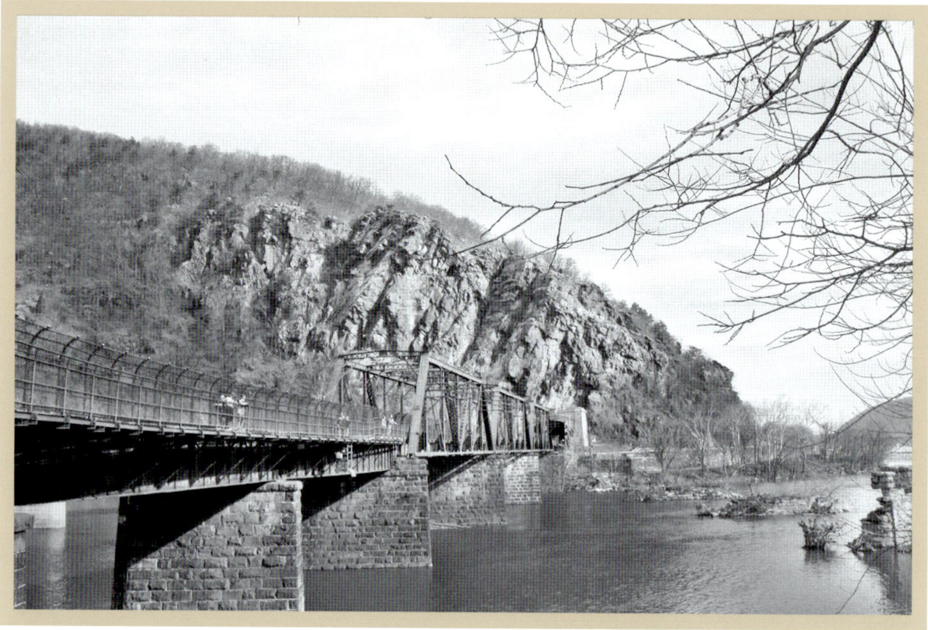

A bollmanized bridge has iron trusses, which make a bridge sturdier and less likely to be damaged or destroyed by floodwaters. In the "then" photograph a bollmanized bridge is pictured at the Point. The west end of the bridge is pictured. The "now" photograph shows that even a bollmanized bridge is not entirely indestructible, although the piers seem to last a long time.

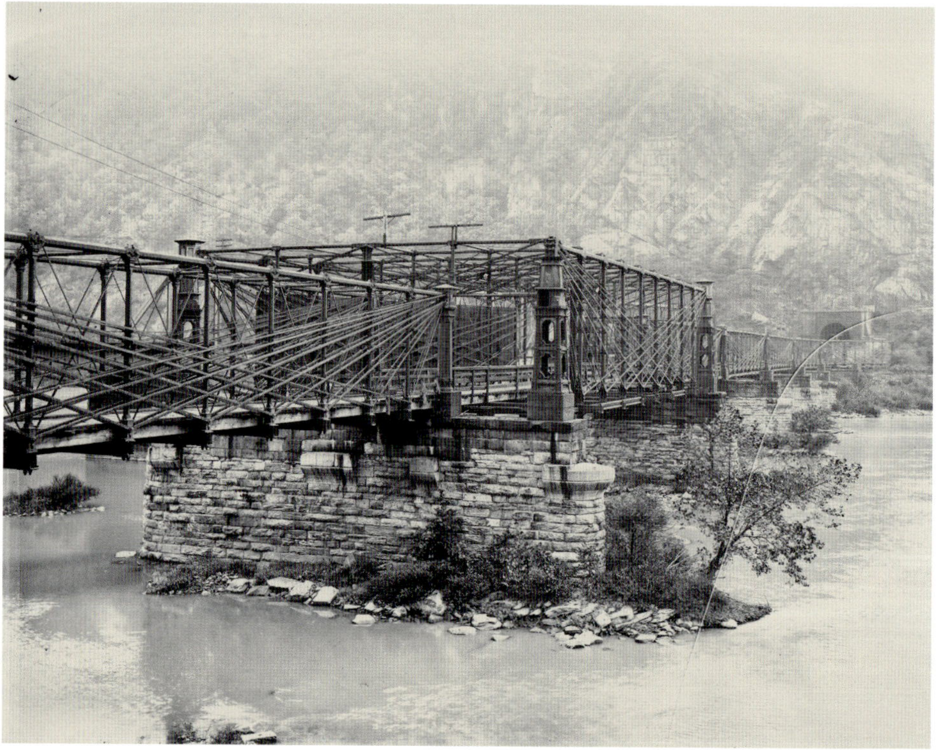

CHAPTER 6

Elevations in Mary's Land

Maryland Heights

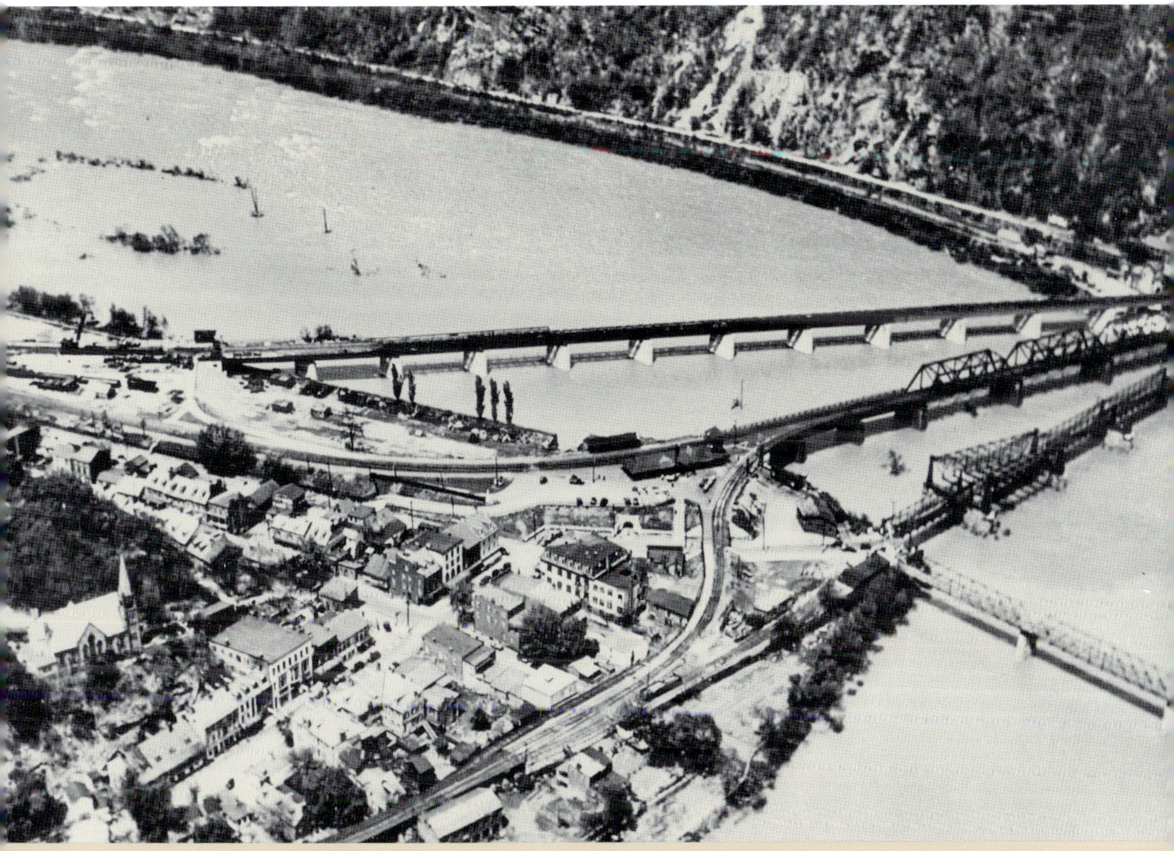

Even though Maryland Heights is technically in the state of Maryland, it is tied forever with Harpers Ferry because of the beautiful views afforded of the town from its top. The Chesapeake and Ohio (C&O) Canal is located at the base of the heights, and that canal played an important role in transportation of both people and supplies to the town, both in peacetime and during the Civil War. Note the high water level

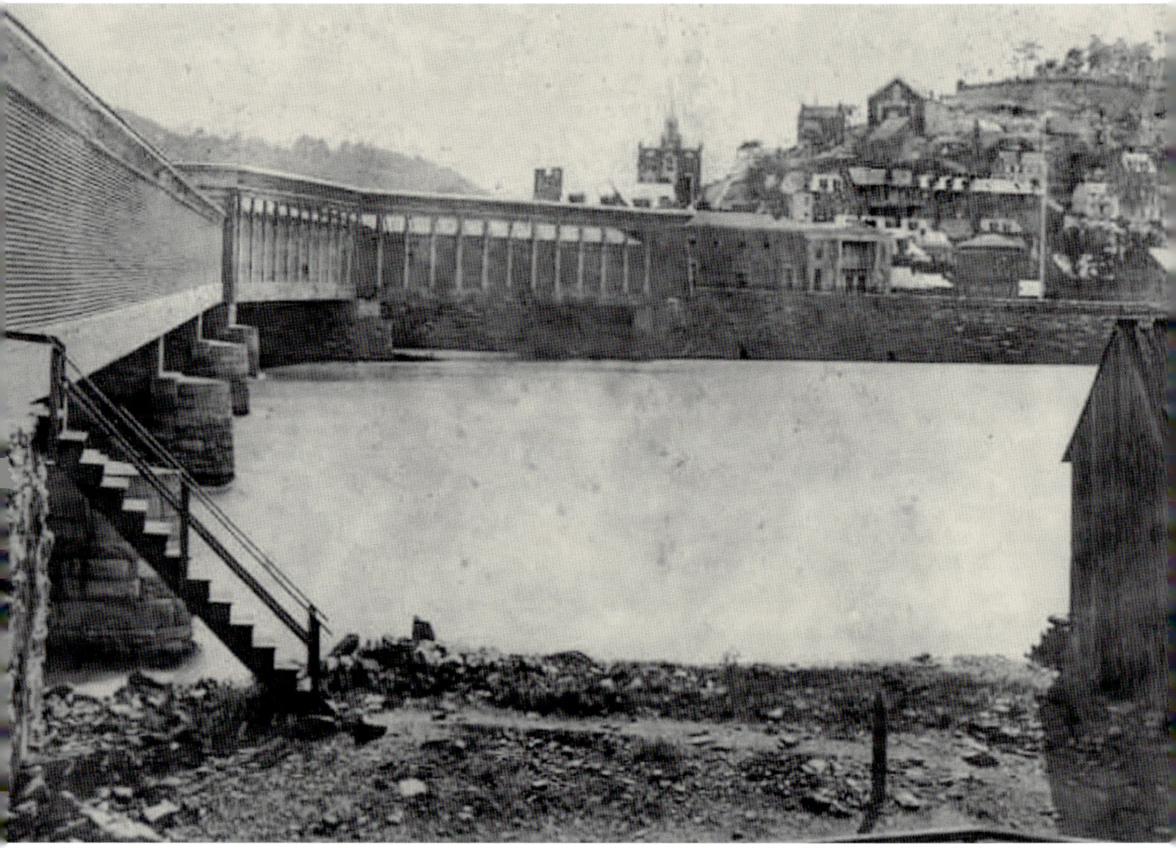

The "then" photograph was taken from the base of Maryland Heights. The bridge had a tin roof and was enclosed with weatherboarding at the time of John Brown's raid, as shown in this photograph. The Catholic and Episcopal churches can be seen in the distance. Today's photograph shows the bridge, no longer covered. In addition, the churches can barely be seen because of the profusion of vegetation.

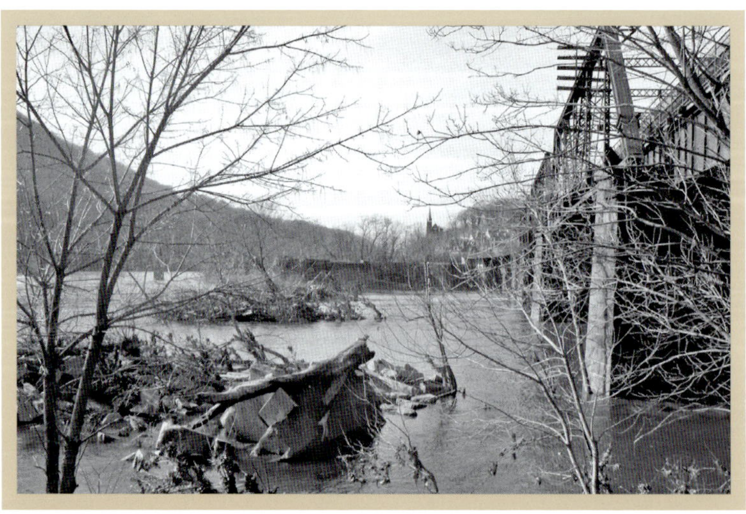

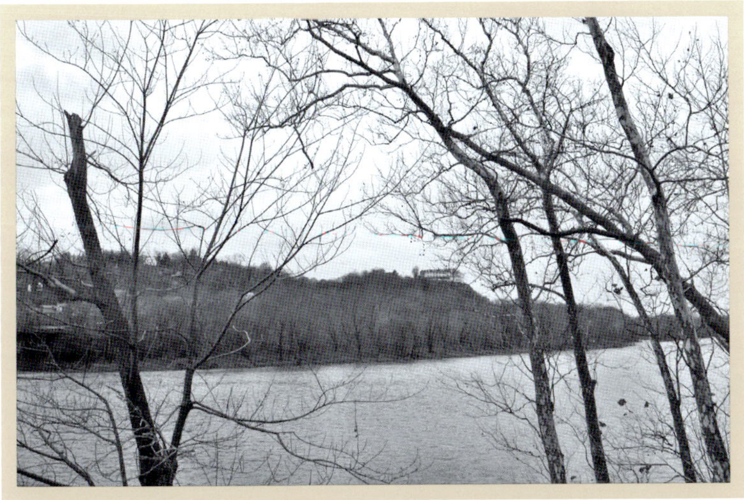

In the distance of the "then" photograph, Camp Hill and Magazine Hill can be seen. W. C. Russell took this photograph between 1882 and 1886. It was taken from the Maryland shore looking at the north end of the Musket Factory Yard. The "now" photograph also shows Camp Hill and Magazine Hill, but vegetation obscures much of the view. The Hilltop House Hotel is visible in the center, slightly to the right.

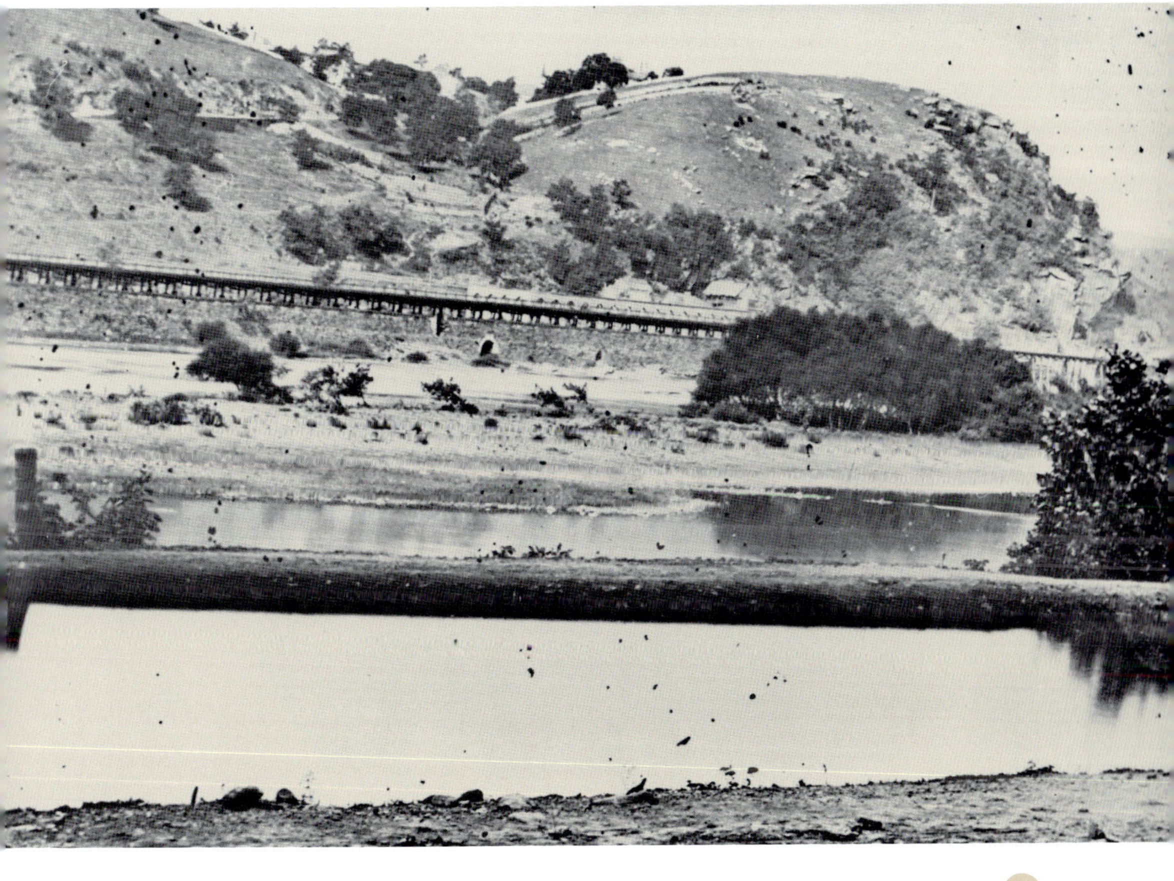

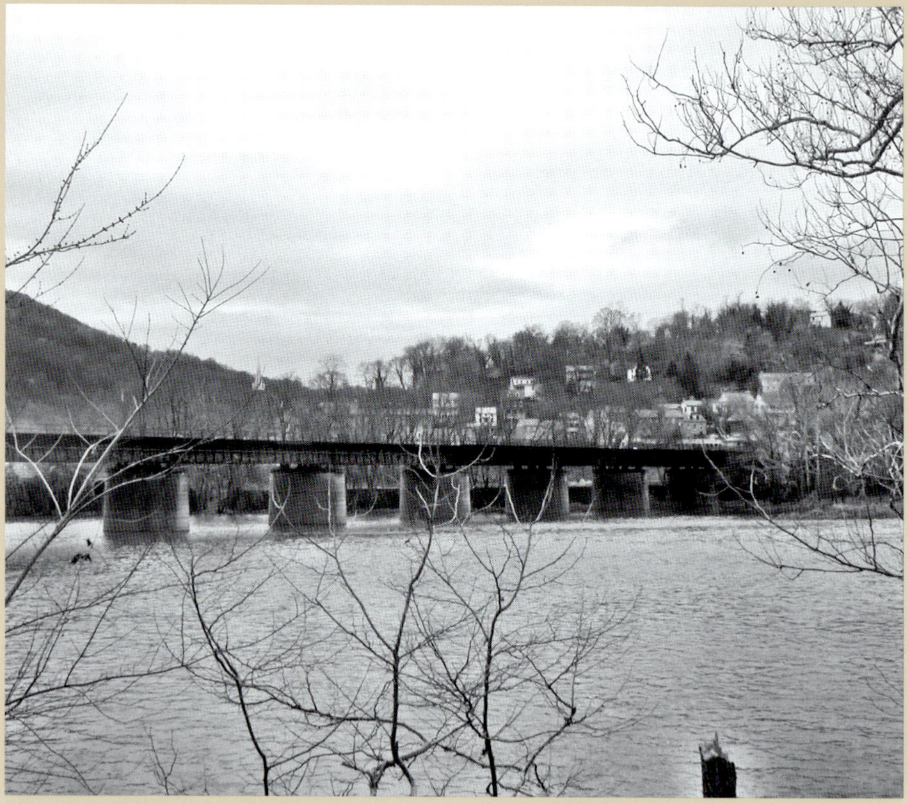

Looking at the "now" photograph, the spire of St. Peter's Catholic Church can be seen to the left of the center. In the "then" photograph, which was taken between 1870 and 1881, the church is much more easily recognizable. In addition, St. John's Protestant Episcopal Church is readily visible. In both photographs, Loudoun Heights is visible on the left side.

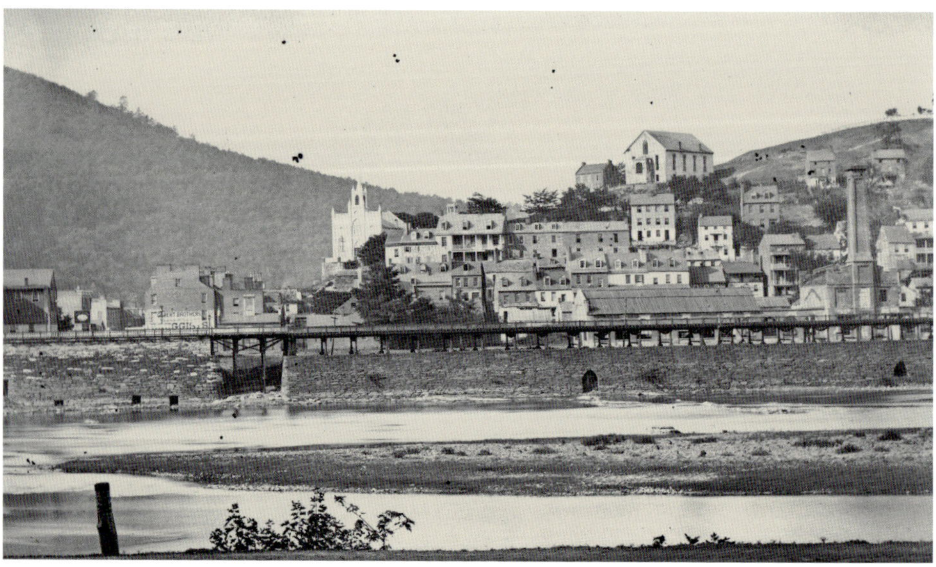

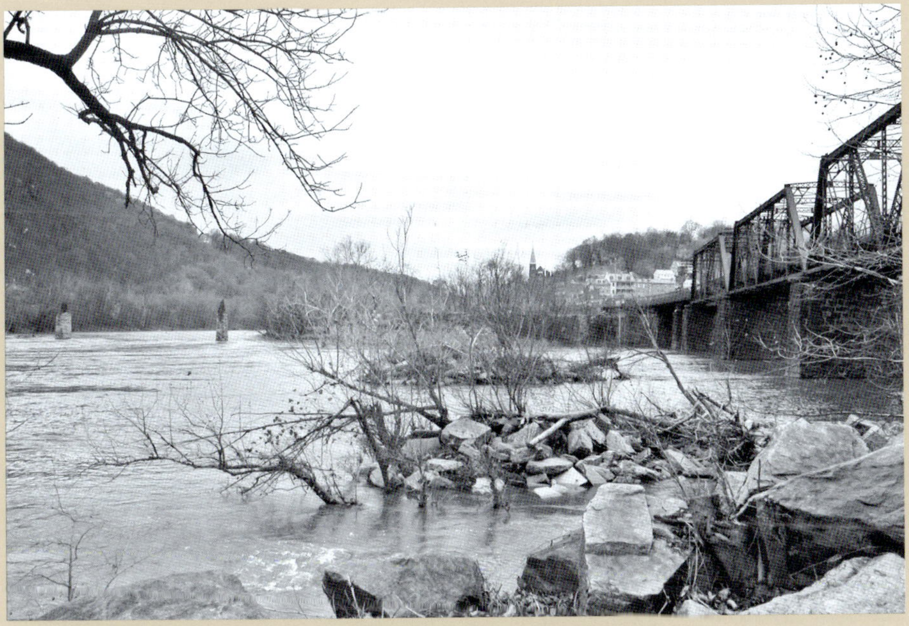

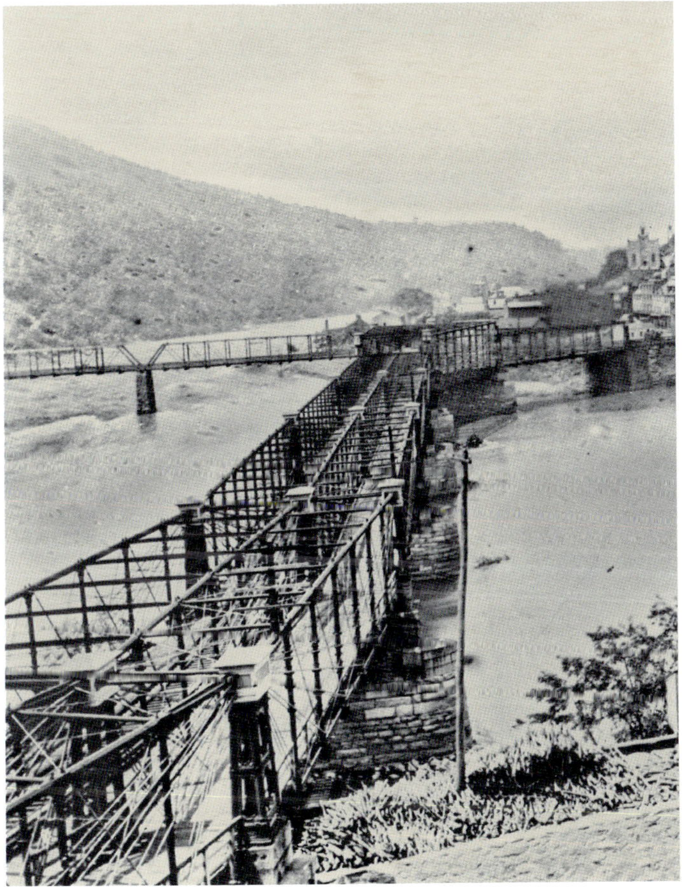

Finding a "then" photograph of the Shenandoah Bridge posed quite a challenge. However, this photograph, taken from Maryland Heights between 1880 and 1890, shows both the metal bridges intact. In the "now" photograph, both bridges are but memories, as only the piers of the bridges are visible in the center and on the left. Bridges across the Shenandoah River seemed to have a shorter lifespan than the Potomac bridges.

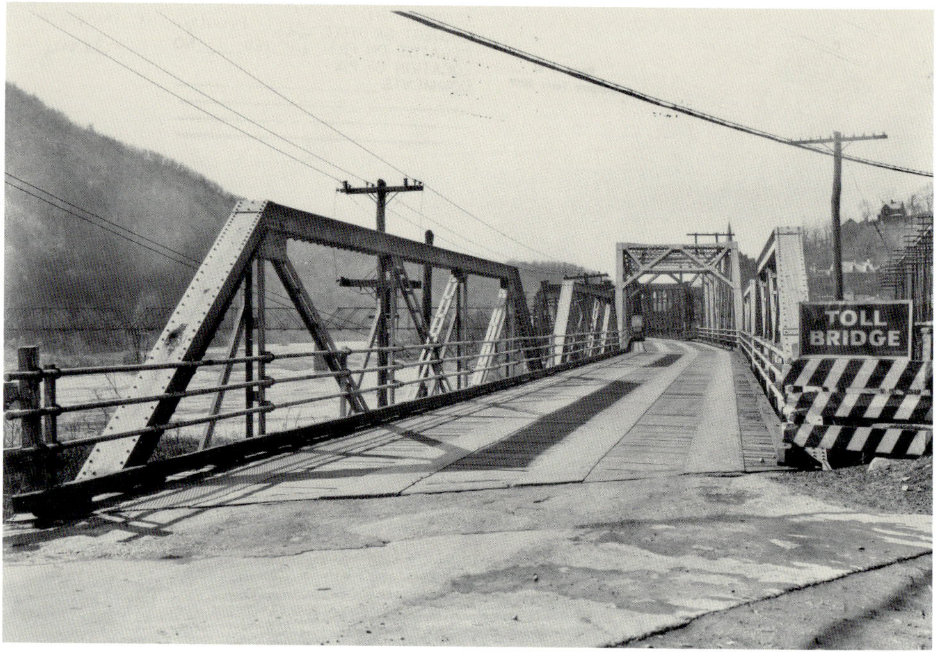

The Potomac River Toll Bridge is pictured in this 1933 photograph. On the right of the photograph is the edge of another bridge. The speed limit for vehicles on this bridge was eight miles per hour. Today the bridge no longer exists, with only the supports visible. Also visible in the "now" photograph is the edge of the railroad bridge on the right.

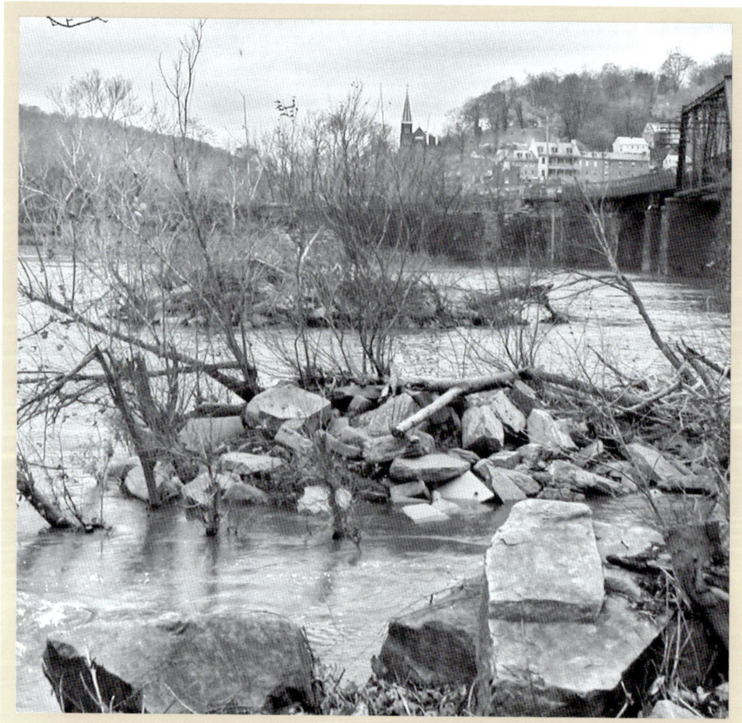

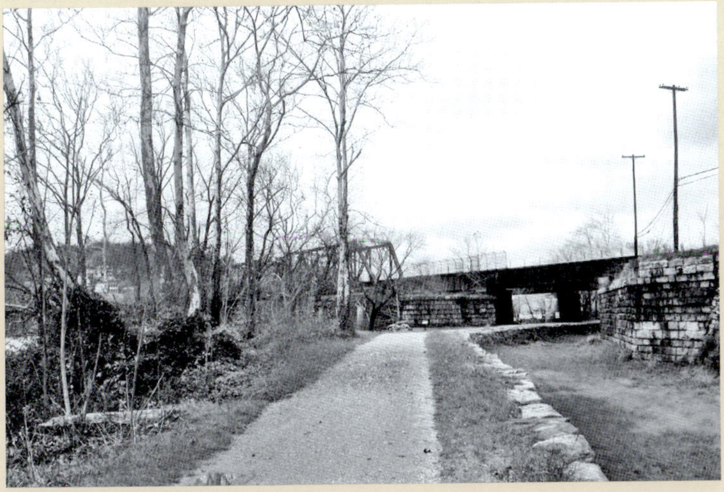

A slightly different view of the Potomac River Toll Bridge is shown in this "then" photograph. Taken in the 1930s, it shows water in the C&O Canal. The same view today shows the railroad bridge, but the toll bridge is no longer in existence. In addition, there is no water in the C&O Canal. The C&O Canal served as an important transportation network between 1790 and 1860.

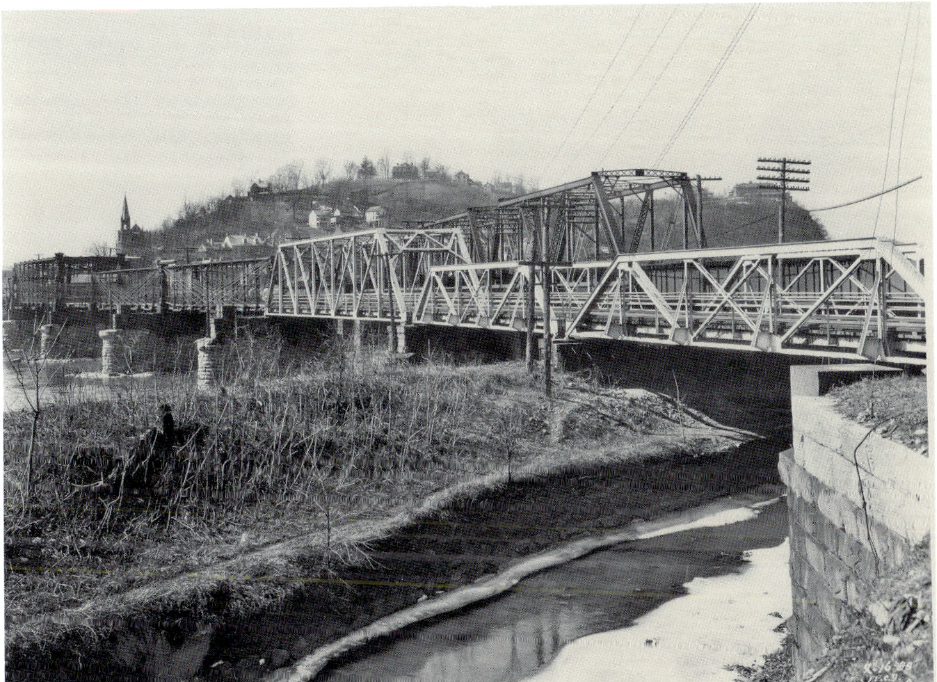

In this "then" photograph can be seen the rocky edge of Maryland Heights. In the "now" photograph, the edge looks every bit as rugged as it does in the older photograph. Harpers shale makes up the composition of the cliffs overhead. If a climber is able to ascend the cliffs of Maryland Heights, a lovely, expansive view of the convergence of the Potomac and Shenandoah Rivers is the visual treasure. The trail from the Point in Harpers Ferry to the summit measures 4.1 rugged miles.

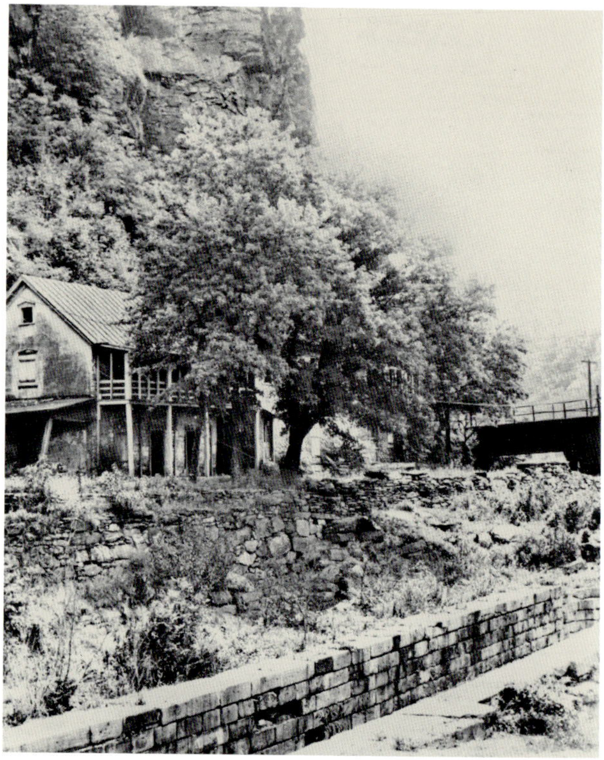

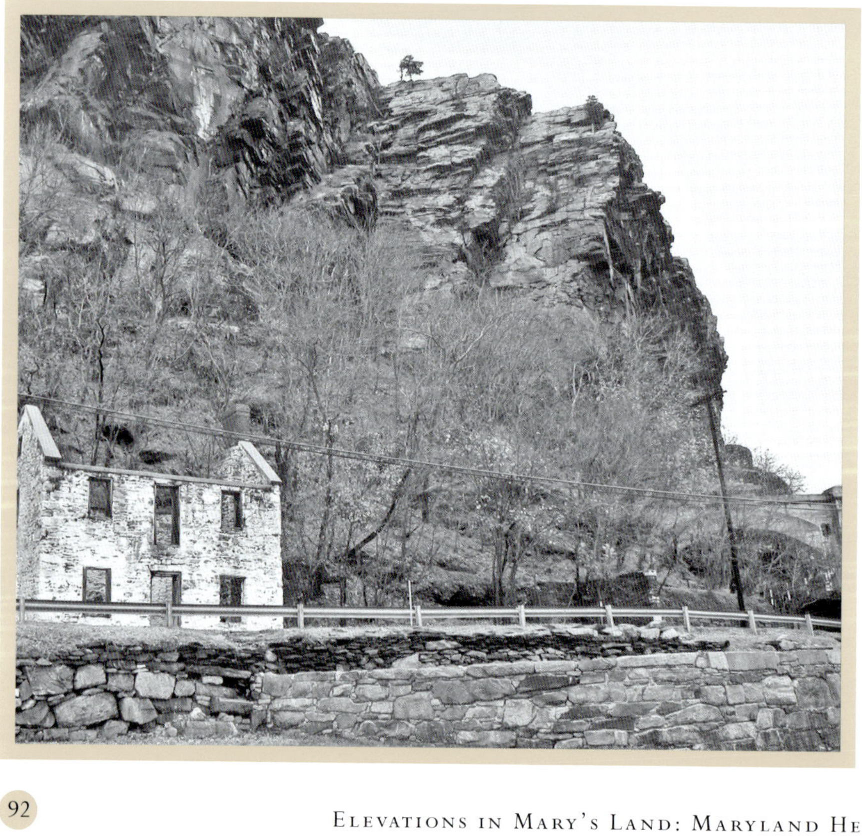

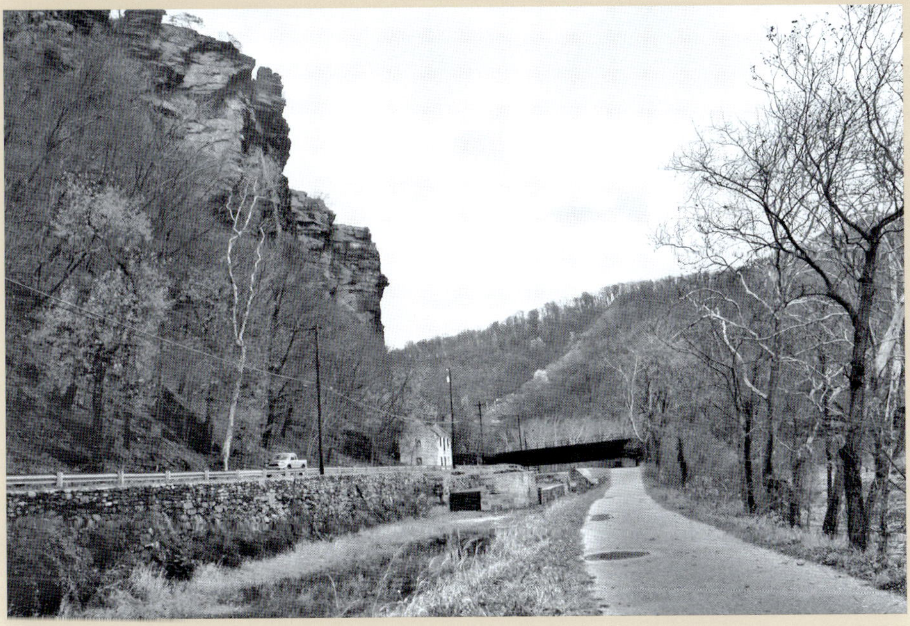

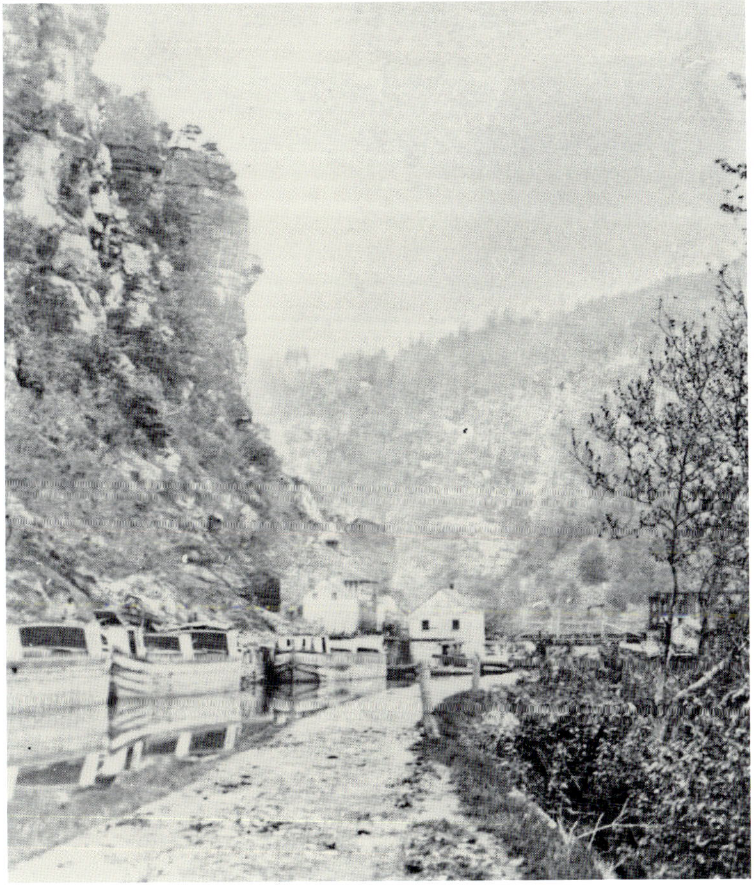

The 1866 photograph shows the C&O Canal at the base of Maryland Heights, looking southeast. Boats are visible in the canal. The boats averaged between 60 and 80 feet long and were usually 14 feet wide, a little smaller than the width of the canal itself, although these sizes varied somewhat. The "now" photograph shows water in the canal but not nearly deep enough to navigate. To the right of the canal is the towpath, on which the mules would walk towing the boats.

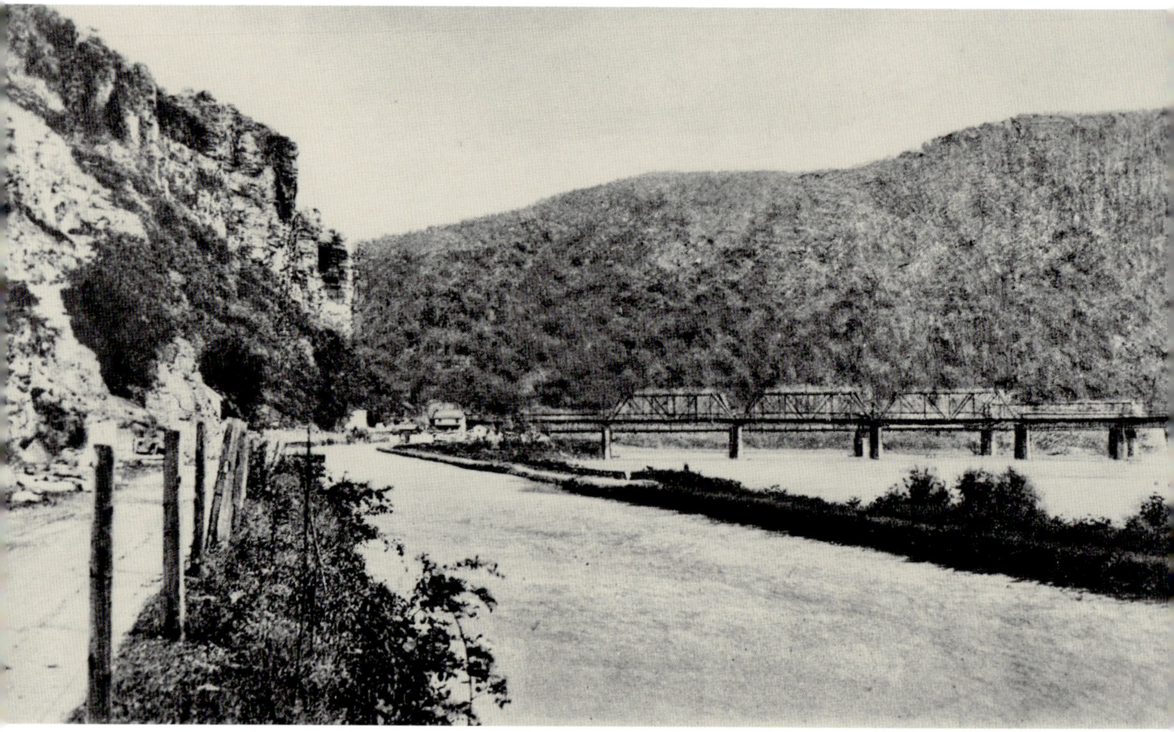

Loudoun Heights is visible in the distance of this *c.* 1915 photograph from the base of Maryland Heights. In the foreground is the old Harpers Ferry Road. The rugged cliffs of Maryland Heights appear to be touching Loudoun Heights, although a river separates them. The modern photograph shows just about the same view except that the bridge has changed over the years.

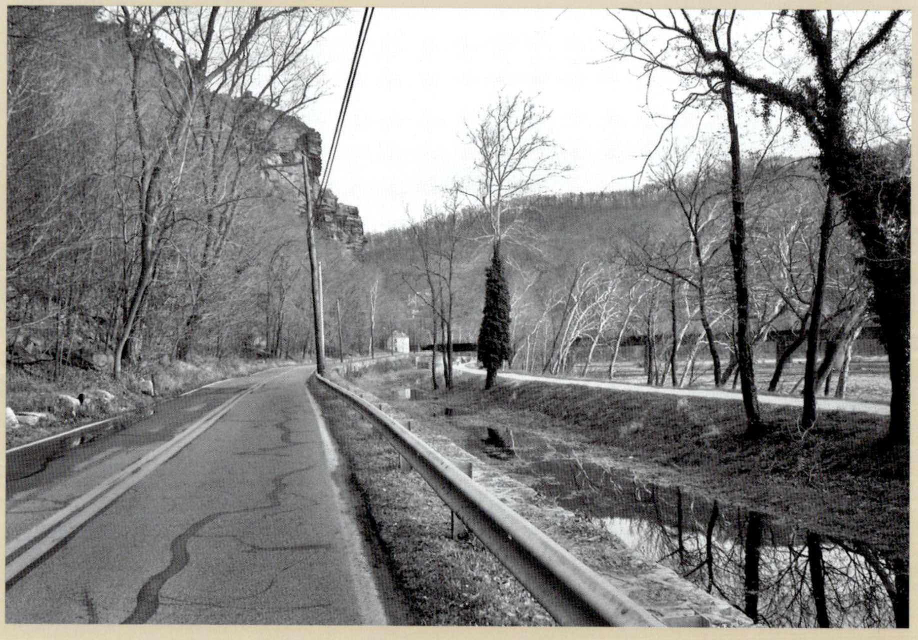

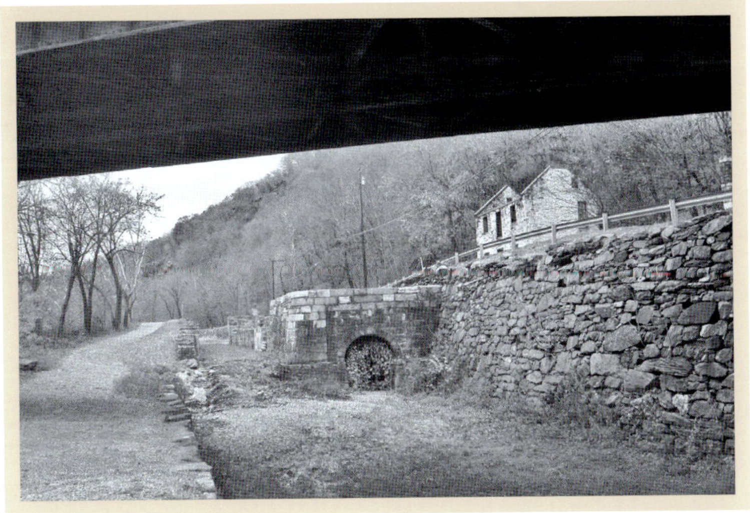

This *c.* 1876 photograph shows Lift Lock 33 of the C&O Canal, located at the base of Maryland Heights. It was completed in 1833, and the walls were constructed of mainly Virginia flint brought from a quarry one and a half miles away. The walls of a stone house can be seen above the canal and slightly to the right. This house was built between 1840 and 1841. In its day, the C&O Canal system was the latest and greatest. Today it is a reminder and relic of times gone by.

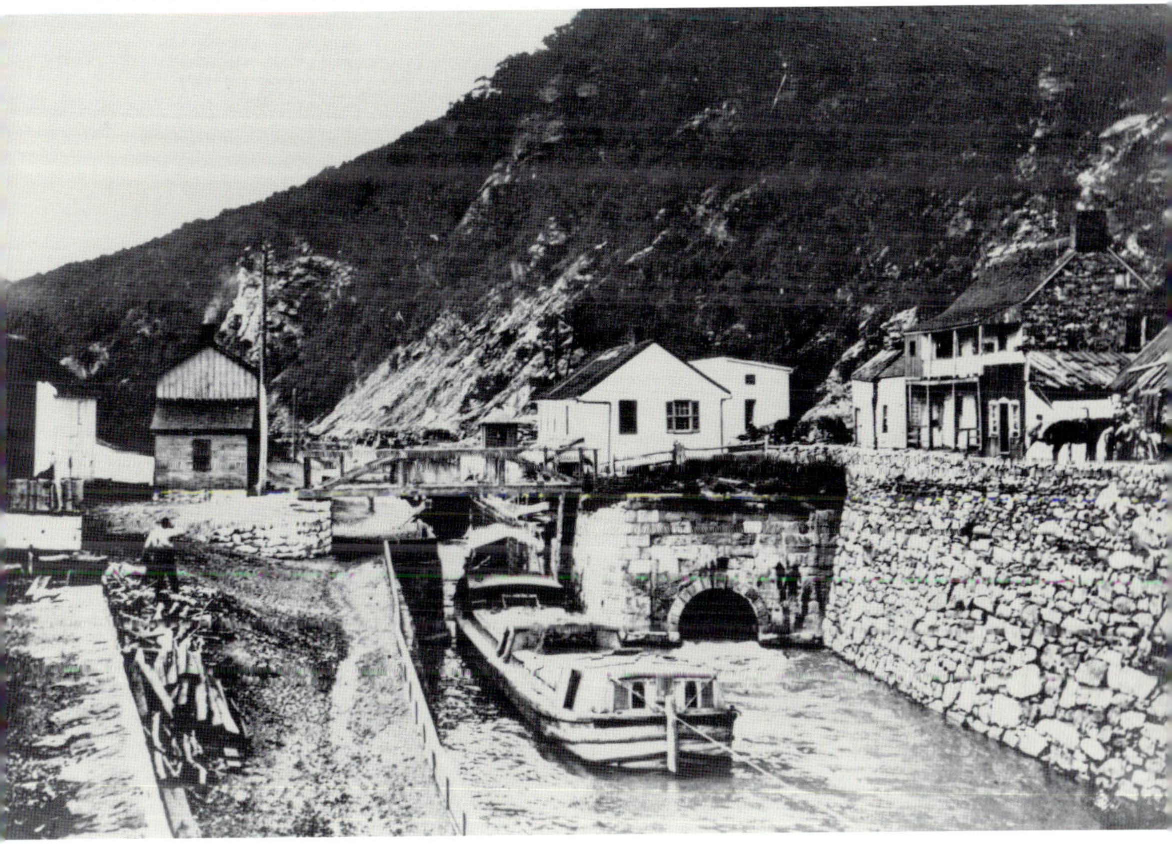